Instructor's Manual and Test Bank to Accompany

— FOURTH EDITION —

TEN STEPS
to
BUILDING
COLLEGE
READING SKILLS

John Langan
ATLANTIC CAPE COMMUNITY COLLEGE

**For book orders and requests for desk copies or supplements,
contact us in any of the following ways:**

By telephone: 1-800-772-6410
By fax: 1-800-225-8894
By e-mail: cs@townsendpress.com
Through our website: www.townsendpress.com

Instructor's Manual and Test Bank to Accompany
Ten Steps to Building College Reading Skills, Fourth Edition
ISBN 1-59194-045-1
9 8 7 6 5 4 3 2 1

CONTENTS

MODEL NOTES AND ADDITIONAL ACTIVITIES FOR "THREE ADDITIONAL READINGS"   43

TEST BANKS AND ANSWERS   55

First Test Bank (Mastery Tests A–D)   57

Note: There are four mastery tests for each skill, similar in format to the six mastery tests in the book itself. These tests can be used at a variety of points along the student's path of working through the chapter and the mastery tests in the book.

Second Test Bank   151

Note: These tests—two for each skill—each contain ten items. They can be used to supplement the four mastery tests in the First Test Bank.

NOTES FOR INSTRUCTORS

On the inside front cover and the first two pages of the Instructor's Edition of *Ten Steps to Building College Reading Skills*, Fourth Edition, I list some hints for teaching a reading course and for using the book. I add here some other comments.

Using a Class Contract

In the first class of the semester, I explain to students that I regard the course as a serious, professional relationship between them and me. I say that I want them to sign a professional contract for taking the course. I then pass out a contract for them to read and sign.

In my experience, the contract helps motivate younger students in particular to come to class and to assume responsibility for their own learning. Some of the older students don't need such a contract, but they welcome a clear presentation of basic ground rules regarding attendance and grading in the course.

A copy of the contract appears on pages 6–7; you have permission to modify and use this contract in whatever way you see fit.

Supplements for the Book

There are four supplements for the book:

1. The *Instructor's Edition,* which is identical to the student book except that it provides the answers to all of the practices and tests. Brief explanations of many answers are also included.

2. The combined *Instructor's Manual and Test Bank* which you are now reading.

3. *Online exercises,* available at the "Online Exercises" section of our website (**www.townsendpress.com**). These exercises are different from any in this manual; they consist of 22 tests, two for each skill and two combined-skills tests.

4. *Downloadable computer software,* in Windows and Macintosh formats. These software tests are identical to the online exercises. (Instructors whose students cannot access the Internet—or who prefer that their students take the computer tests in a supervised computer lab—can download these tests at the "For Teachers" section of our website.)

If you've adopted the book for use in your reading classes, you're entitled to free copies of these supplements. Call us at 1-800-772-6410, send a fax to 1-800-225-8894, or e-mail us at <cs@townsendpress.com> to get them shipped out to you immediately.

1

A Suggested Syllabus

Weeks 1–10:

One way to begin using the book is to have students work through the activities in "How to Become a Better Reader and Thinker" on pages 23–30. Then, as the first homework assignment, ask them to read "Getting Off to a Strong Start" on pages 3–13 and the essay "One Reader's Story" on pages 15–22, and urge them to take advantage of the book offer on pages 12–13. In the next class, discuss the questions on page 22; you may wish to ask students to write a paper on one of the questions as well.

I suggest then teaching one chapter a week, following the order in the book. Generally at the end of a chapter I give two tests: one for practice and one that counts for a grade.

I go over the tests in class right after students take them. (I recommend collecting test papers as students finish and distributing them to students in other parts of the room. Some students resist putting X's on a paper that belongs to the person sitting right next to them.) That way students get immediate feedback on how they have done. Also, after class all I need to do is to check the grades quickly and transfer them to my grade book.

As the semester progresses, I use additional mastery tests, every so often, to review skills covered previously in the class.

Weeks 11–15:

In the last five weeks, students read two selections a week from Part II of the book. They also do the remaining tests, including some of those in this manual.

Having done all of the reading of the materials in the book, as well as all of the thinking required to complete the many activities, students are, in my experience, better readers and thinkers. They are better equipped both to handle a standardized reading test at the semester's end and to go on to content courses in their college curriculum.

Suggested Answers to the Discussion Questions

Pages 23–42 in this manual provide suggested answers to the discussion questions that follow each of the twenty readings in Parts I and II of the book. There was simply no room in the *Instructor's Edition* for this material.

Writing Assignments

Writing and reading are closely related skills: practice at one will make a student better at the other. Also, writing about a selection is an excellent way of thinking about it. For these reasons, writing assignments are provided (beginning on page 570 of the book) for each of the twenty readings in Parts I and II.

If you ask students to write about a selection, I suggest you first have them read the "Brief Guide to Effective Writing," which appears on pages 568–569.

Teaching Vocabulary

One basic change that I've made in my teaching of reading is that I now directly teach vocabulary. We all know that students don't know enough words. Because they don't, they have trouble understanding what they read, and they're limited in what they can write. (We have all seen how, in standardized reading tests, students are frustrated because they don't know enough of the words in a passage to understand it and to answer comprehension questions about it. And we all know that because of the vocabulary problem, the standardized tests that are intended to measure reading comprehension are often in fact serving as vocabulary tests.)

I teach vocabulary using a words-in-context approach (it is of no value to ask students to memorize isolated lists of vocabulary words). Specifically, I use a book titled *Building Vocabulary Skills, Short Version*, by Sherrie Nist and Carole Mohr. There are twenty chapters in this book, with ten words in each chapter. I do the first chapter in class, so that students understand how to use the pronunciation key for the words and understand just how the chapter works. I then assign one or two chapters a week for homework.

In class each week, I walk around and check students' books to see that they have worked through the material for each chapter. (After this quick check, we then return the focus of the class to reading skills.) Every third week, I give students one of the several unit tests that follow each unit of five chapters in the book. My vocabulary syllabus for *Building Vocabulary Skills, Short Version* looks like this:

Week 2:   Vocabulary chapter 1 covered in class
Week 3:   Vocabulary chapters 2–3 for homework
Week 4:   Vocabulary chapters 4–5 for homework plus a test on Unit One in class
Week 5:   Vocabulary chapters 6–7 for homework
Week 6:   Vocabulary chapters 8–9 for homework
Week 7:   Vocabulary chapter 10 for homework plus a test on Unit Two in class
Week 8:   Vocabulary chapters 11–12 for homework
Week 9:   Vocabulary chapters 13–14 for homework
Week 10: Vocabulary chapter 15 for homework plus a test on Unit Three in class
Week 11: Vocabulary chapters 16–17 for homework
Week 12: Vocabulary chapters 18–19 for homework
Week 13: Vocabulary chapter 20 for homework plus a test on Unit Four in class

The Importance of Continual Reading and Thinking

Continual reading—coupled with thinking about what one has read—is the very heart of a reading class. *One improves the skills of reading and thinking through guided reading and thinking.* This statement is emphasized with good reason. If a teacher is not careful, he or she may play too participatory a role in the classroom, getting more reading and thinking practice than the student does. The teacher should serve as a manager, using the materials in the text to give students the skills practice they need. *Ten Steps to Building College Reading Skills* helps the teacher ensure that students do a great deal of active reading and thinking in the classroom.

The Importance of Constant Feedback

Along with continual reading, writing, and thinking, it is vital that students get frequent feedback. Here are ways they can secure such feedback:

- Small-group interactions
- Class discussions and reviews
- Short one-on-one sessions with the teacher
- Graded quizzes and tests
- Use of the limited answer key in the back of the book
- The online exercises available at **www.townsendpress.com**

In addition, since instructors using *Ten Steps to Building College Reading Skills* as a class text are permitted to reproduce any or all parts of this manual, you can selectively hand out copies of answers included here.

All of the exercises in the book are designed to make it easy to give clear and specific feedback. If students are going to learn to read and think more effectively, then they need clear, logical, specific responses to their efforts. This book enables teachers to provide such feedback.

Outlining, Mapping, and Summarizing

To take thoughtful, effective study notes, students need to learn three essential techniques: outlining, mapping, and summarizing. The three techniques often require students to identify the main idea and the major supporting details of a selection. But while educators agree that these three techniques are important for students to learn, they are too seldom taught.

The book gives students instruction and practice in the three techniques. Passages in the "Supporting Details" and the two "Relationships" chapters, as well as all of the reading selections in Part II, are followed by an outline, a map, or a summary activity. To complete many of these activities, students must look closely at the basic organization of the selection. They must think carefully about what they have read by asking two key questions: "What is the point?" and "What is the support for that point?" As students apply the techniques from one selection to the next and get specific feedback on their efforts, they will develop their ability to think in a clear and logical way.

Readability Levels . . . and Their Limitations

Below are the readability grade levels for the text of the book itself and the twenty reading selections. Because the book has been prepared on a computer, and there are now software programs that determine readability, it has been possible to do a complete readability evaluation for each reading, rather than merely sampling excerpts from the materials.

Please remember, however, that there are limits to the reliability and validity of readability scores. For instance, a readability formula cannot account for such significant factors as student interest, prior knowledge of a subject, the number of examples provided to explain concepts, and the overall clarity and logic of the writing.

Thus, while "Responsibility" has a readability level of 6th grade, it is a sophisticated adult piece that may be more challenging to students than, for example, "Disaster and Friendship," which has a reading level of 8. I respect readability levels, but I also take them with a grain of salt, and I have kept other factors in mind while determining the sequence of readings.

Material	Word Count	Reading Level
Text of *Ten Steps to Building College Reading Skills*		8

Material	Word Count	Reading Level
Part I		
1. Responsibility	724	6
2. All the Good Things	1161	5
3. Group Pressure	937	7
4. Touch Sparks Love	2017	5
5. Body Language	1335	9
6. Behind Closed Doors: Violence in the Family	1206	9
7. The Most Hateful Words	614	5
8. Half a Pound of Ham	1088	5
9. Lighting a Match	1148	7
10. Do It Better!	2982	6
Part II		
1. Winners, Losers, or Just Kids?	746	10
2. The Storyteller	1734	6
3. Disaster and Friendship	1661	8
4. Read All About It	1443	6
5. Adult Children at Home	1383	8
6. How to Make It in College, Now That You're Here	2640	7
7. False Ideas About Reading	1250	8
8. Are You a Good Listener?	2247	8
9. Dealing with Feelings	1661	10
10. Childhood Stress and Resilience	1339	10

A Final Note

Writing a book that contains hundreds of explanations and activities is a bit like being in a ball game where one steps up to the batter's box an almost countless number of times. One tries to get as many hits and extra-base hits as possible: to explain every concept so that students really understand it; to provide readings and practices that both interest students and teach the skills. One tries not to hit any foul balls. Hopefully there are not too many in this Fourth Edition of a book that has benefited from a lot of teacher and student feedback.

Realistically, though, you might find that despite my best efforts, some items may not work. If they don't, and/or if you or your students are confused or uncertain about certain items, let me know so that I can consider making changes in the next printing or revision of the book. To do so, call Townsend Press at its toll-free number: 1-800-772-6410; send a fax to 1-800-225-8894; or send e-mail to <cs@townsendpress.com>; your comments will be passed on to me. And if you have a question, a Townsend editor will get back to you with an answer very shortly. My thanks in advance for your help in my effort to keep improving the book!

John Langan

A PROFESSIONAL CONTRACT

FOR FIFTEEN WEEKS TOGETHER

between

_____

(Student's name here)

and

_____

(Instructor's name here)

Welcome to *(name of course)* _____. Counting today, we will be spending fifteen weeks together, for two and a half hours every week. To show your commitment to the course, you are asked to read and sign the following contract. I will then sign it and return it to you. Here are the terms of the contract.

MY ROLE IN THE CONTRACT

My role will be to help you practice and master important reading and writing and thinking and learning skills. I will try to present these communication skills clearly and to give you interesting and worthwhile practice materials. I will conduct this as a skills course—not a lecture course where you could borrow a friend's notes afterwards. Typically several skills will be explained briefly in class, and you will then spend most of the class time in practicing those skills, making them your own. You will be learning in the best possible way: through doing.

Why learn these skills?

I promise you that the skills will be of real value to you in all the other courses you take in college. They will make you a better reader, writer, thinker, and learner, and they can dramatically increase your chance for success in school.

The skills can be just as valuable for the career work you are likely to do in the years ahead. Consider that America is no longer an industrial society where many people work on farms or in factories. Instead, most jobs now involve providing services or processing information. More than ever, communication skills are the tools of our trade. This course will be concerned directly with helping you learn and strengthen the communication skills that will be vital for job success in the twenty-first century.

YOUR ROLE IN THE CONTRACT

Experiencing the course

Your role in this contract will be to come to every class and to give a full effort. Much of the value and meaning of this skills course will come from what happens in class, so you must be here on a steady basis. Imagine trying to learn another skill without being present: for example, imagine learning how to drive without the *experience* of actually being in the car and working with the controls and getting feedback from your instructor. How much would you learn about the skill of driving if you relied only on the notes of a classmate? In a similar way, to really learn communication skills, you need direct experience and practice. So if you miss classes, then, you are in effect missing the course.

6

Shaping your attitude

Some people start college with a "high-school mindset." They are passive; they do the minimum they need to get by; their attention is elsewhere; they are like the living dead—and the American high-school system (and watching thousands of hours of television) may be to blame. Gradually these people realize that college is not high school: they don't have to be in college, and they are no longer part of the sad game played out in many high schools, where they receive a free ride and promotion no matter how little they do.

If your attitude about learning has been hurt by what happened in high school, then part of your role is to change your attitude. You can do so, and this contract will help.

Understanding sick days and personal days

You should try not to miss *any* classes. But in the professional environment of this class, like in the work world, everyone is entitled to a set number of sick days as well as "personal days"— unexplained absences. In this course, you will have a total of *(insert number)* _____ such days— which can cover such real-world happenings as sickness, car breakdowns, or even the death of someone you know. If you missed more than this amount of time in a real-world job contract, you would be let go. (Only in some extraordinary situation, such as an extended illness confirmed by a doctor's report, might an exception apply.) The professional terms of the work world will apply here: if you miss more than _____ classes, you cannot pass the course.

YOUR ROLE IF YOU MISS CLASS

If you do miss a class, you are responsible for getting the homework for the following week's class. To do so, call a classmate. Write down the names and phone numbers of two people in the room. (For now, use the people sitting on either side of you; you can always change these names later.)

Classmate # 1: *Name* _____   *Phone* _____

Classmate # 2: *Name* _____   *Phone* _____

Note that you **must** turn in all homework assignments or you **cannot pass the course**.

If a test or tests are given on a day you miss class, you cannot ordinarily make up these tests. Instead, you will receive a grade of M (Missing) for each missed test. When all your grades are averaged at the end of the semester, three M's will be omitted; the rest will convert to zeros.

YOUR COMMITMENT

I've read this contract, and the terms seem fair to me. (I like the fact that this college class is being treated as a professional situation, and I'm learning the ground rules up front.) I accept the responsibility and the challenge to make this course worth my time and money.

_____   _____

Signed by (your name here)   *Date*

_____

Witnessed by the instructor

OR: If you don't want to sign this, please meet with me after this class to talk about why.

ANSWERS TO THE TESTS IN THE BOOK

Answers to the Review and Mastery Tests in Part I

DICTIONARY USE:
Review Test 1

1. B   4. A
2. C   5. E
3. A

DICTIONARY USE:
Review Test 2

A. 1. O   **C.** 11. determination
2. B   12. savor
3. F   13. humanize
4. O   14. profile
5. O   15. lunatic
B. 6. cabinet   16. humanize
7. circus   17. Second
8. design   18. First
9. gingerbread   19. Fourth
10. dynamite   20. Five

DICTIONARY USE:
Mastery Test 1

A. 1. B   **B.** 11. freeze
2. 3   12. tendency
3. A   13. parallel
4. B   14. tuna
5. A   15. accelerate
6. C   **C.** 16. im•pose ĭm-pōz′
7. 3   17. sa•dis•tic sə-dĭs′tĭk
8. A   18. in•ev•i•ta•ble
9. C   ĭn-ĕv′ĭ-tə-bəl
10. C   19. ap•pre•hen•sive
                ăp′rĭ-hĕn′sĭv
          20. ster•e•o•type
                stĕr′ē-ə-tīp′

DICTIONARY USE:
Mastery Test 4

A. 1. B   **B.** 11. verb, noun
2. B   12. verb, noun, adjective
3. A   13. verb, noun, adjective
4. 2   14. verb, adjective
5. 1   15. noun, verb
6. B   **C.** 16. strategies
7. A   17. alumni
8. A   18. mothers-in-law
9. 1   19. crises
10. 2   20. passers-by (*or* passersby)

DICTIONARY USE:
Review Test 3

A. 1. scape•goat skāp′gōt′
2. ex•haust ĭg-zôst′
3. de•ci•sion dĭ-sĭzh′ən
4. cel•e•brate sĕl′ə-brāt′
5. re•cip•ro•cate rĭ-sĭp′rə-kāt′
B. 6. noun, verb
7. noun, verb
8. memories
9. livelier, liveliest
10. to drench thoroughly or cover with or as if with a liquid

DICTIONARY USE:
Mastery Test 2

A. 1. A   **B.** 11. supplement
2. 3   12. retrieve
3. A   13. pessimist
4. B   14. illuminate
5. C   15. inevitable
6. A   **C.** 16. as•pire ə-spīr′
7. 3   17. en•coun•ter
8. C   ĕn-koun′tər
9. B   18. prin•ci•pal prĭn′sə-pəl
10. B   19. ter•mi•nate
                tûr′mə-nāt′
          20. i•mag•i•na•tion
                ĭ-măj′ə-nā′shən

DICTIONARY USE:
Mastery Test 5

(Wording of definitions may vary.)

1. nŏk-tûr′nəl; most active at night
2. rē-hə-bĭl′ĭ-tāt′; to restore to good health or active life
3. dĭ-môr′ə-līz′ĭs; undermines the confidence or morale of
4. ĭm-pōz′ĭs; takes unfair advantage
5. mûr′sə-nĕr′ē; motivated by a desire for monetary or material gain
6. kər-tāld′; cut short
7. sə-sĕp′tə-bəl; likely to be affected (with)
8. plô′zə-bəl; seemingly or apparently valid, likely, or acceptable
9. străt′ə-jē; a plan of action intended to accomplish a specific goal
10. ĭn-ĕk′wĭ-tē; injustice; unfairness

DICTIONARY USE:
Review Test 4

1. ə-mē′nə-bəl *or* ə-mĕn′ə-bəl
2. Second
3. Adjective
4. lōō′dĭ-krəs
5. First
6. Verb
7. re•spon•si•bil•i•ty (6 syllables)
8. id•i•ot•i•cal•ly (6 syllables)
9. A
10. A

DICTIONARY USE:
Mastery Test 3

A. 1. B   **B.** 11. exercise
2. B   12. deceive
3. B   13. finally
4. 2   14. gullible
5. 1   15. persistent
6. B   **C.** 16. e•lapse ĭ-lăps′
7. 2   17. du•bi•ous dōō′bē-əs
8. A   18. an•ti•dote ăn′tĭ-dōt′
9. 1   19. in•gen•ious
10. 2   ĭn-jēn′yəs
          20. per•se•ver•ance
                pûr′sə-vîr′əns

DICTIONARY USE:
Mastery Test 6

(Wording of definitions may vary.)

1. ĭ-lĕj′ə-bəl; not able to be read or deciphered
2. dĭ-spûrs′; to move in different directions; scatter
3. yōō-năn′ə-məs; based on or characterized by complete agreement
4. prə-pĕld′; caused to move forward
5. fĭs′kəl; of or relating to finance or finances
6. prŏp′ə-găn′də; material disseminated by advocates of a doctrine or cause
7. nŏm′ə-nəl; insignificantly small; trifling
8. ĭ-lōō′mə-nāt′; to provide or brighten with light
9. ôl′tərd; changed or made different; modified
10. ə-rĭj′ə-nāt′ĭd; came into being; started

9

VOCABULARY IN CONTEXT:
Review Test 1

   1. C   4. C
   2. A   5. A
   3. B

VOCABULARY IN CONTEXT:
Review Test 2

A. 1. B   **C.** 6. D violations
B. 2. C   7. E warning
     3. C   8. C lazy
     4. D   9. A messy
     5. B   10. B clear and
                       brief

VOCABULARY IN CONTEXT:
Review Test 3

A. 1. A
B. 2. D small
     3. A reward
     4. G encourage
     5. J expensive
C. 6. F catch and eat
     7. A attracts
     8. C closes
     9. I explore
    10. G danger

VOCABULARY IN CONTEXT:
Review Test 4

   1. B   6. A
   2. D   7. B
   3. A   8. C
   4. B   9. A
   5. C   10. B

VOCABULARY IN CONTEXT:
Mastery Test 1

A. 1. Examples: *she missed two weeks of classes because of a strep throat, had all her books stolen just before finals;* A
     2. Examples: *a homeless man caring for a little dog, a woman in a slum growing flowers in a patch of soil;* B
     3. Examples: *firing teachers, forbidding after-school activities;* D
B. 4. show off
     5. signal
     6. fearful
C. 7. Antonym, *dirty;* D
     8. Antonym, *interest;* D
     9. A
    10. D

VOCABULARY IN CONTEXT:
Mastery Test 2

A. 1. Examples: *ignoring his memos, making fun of him behind his back;* D
     2. Examples: *brown spots, soft places, small holes in the skin;* A
     3. make clear
     4. never happened before
     5. die down
B. 6. Antonym, *cheerful;* A
     7. Antonym, *forward;* D
     8. C
     9. B
    10. D

VOCABULARY IN CONTEXT:
Mastery Test 3

   1. A   6. B
   2. C   7. C
   3. D   8. A
   4. B   9. C
   5. C   10. D

VOCABULARY IN CONTEXT:
Mastery Test 4

   1. B   6. B
   2. D   7. C
   3. A   8. D
   4. B   9. C
   5. D   10. B

VOCABULARY IN CONTEXT:
Mastery Test 5

A. 1. A
     2. C
     3. B
     4. B
     5. A
B. 6. H get involved
     7. G dangerous
     8. C discouragement
     9. A inactive
    10. B stand up to

VOCABULARY IN CONTEXT:
Mastery Test 6

A. 1. G highly unusul
     2. F coating
     3. E step forth
     4. C enormous
     5. A drops off
B. 6. fascinating
     7. leaving   *(Wording of*
     8. start   *answers 6–10*
     9. goes back *may vary.)*
    10. job

MAIN IDEAS:
Review Test 1

1. main idea
2. specific
3. topic
4. supported
5. detail

MAIN IDEAS:
Review Test 2

A.
1. position
2. utility
3. housing
4. sense
5. drug
6. ingredient
7. decoration
8. debt

B. *(Answers will vary.)* Possibilities:

9–10. cat, dog
11–12. knife, needle
13–14. aunt, nephew
15–16. toast, coffee

C. A. S
    B. S
    C. P
    D. S

MAIN IDEAS:
Review Test 3

A.

	Group 1	Group 2	Group 3
A.	MI	T	T
B.	SD	SD	SD
C.	SD	MI	MI
D.	T	SD	SD

B. 13. B
   14. 1
   15. B
   16. 3

C. 17. C
   18. C

D. 19. A
   20. B

MAIN IDEAS:
Review Test 4

1. B
2. C
3. A
4. B
5. D
6. C
7. C
8. D
9. A
10. A

MAIN IDEAS:
Mastery Test 1

A.
1. tree
2. metal
3. insect
4. sport

B. *(Answers will vary.)* Possibilities:

5–6. banana, grape
7–8. Mexico, Egypt
9–10. Thanksgiving, Christmas
11–12. murderer, robber

C.

	Group 1	Group 2
A.	S	P
B.	S	S
C.	P	S
D.	S	S

MAIN IDEAS:
Mastery Test 2

A.
1. flower
2. furniture
3. illness
4. clothes

B. *(Answers will vary.)* Possibilities:

5–6. coffee, tea
7–8. canary, pigeon
9–10. flood, forest fire
11–12. getting married, graduation

C.

	Group 1	Group 2
A.	S	S
B.	S	S
C.	P	S
D.	S	P

MAIN IDEAS:
Mastery Test 3

A.

	Group 1	Group 2	Group 3
A.	S	P	S
B.	S	S	S
C.	P	S	S
D.	S	S	P

B.

	Group 1	Group 2
A.	SD	SD
B.	T	SD
C.	SD	MI
D.	MI	T

MAIN IDEAS:
Mastery Test 4

A.

	Group 1	Group 2	Group 3
A.	S	S	S
B.	S	S	P
C.	S	S	S
D.	P	P	S

B.

	Group 1	Group 2
A.	SD	MI
B.	SD	SD
C.	MI	T
D.	T	SD

MAIN IDEAS:
Mastery Test 5

A. (1–4.)

A.	S
B.	S
C.	P
D.	S

B.

	Group 1	Group 2
A.	SD	SD
B.	SD	MI
C.	T	SD
D.	MI	T

C. 13. A
   14. C
   15. C
   16. C

D. 17. B
   18. C
   19. A
   20. C

MAIN IDEAS:
Mastery Test 6

A. (1–4.)

A.	S
B.	S
C.	P
D.	S

B.

	Group 1	Group 2
A.	SD	T
B.	MI	SD
C.	T	SD
D.	SD	MI

C. 13. C
   14. B
   15. C
   16. C

D. 17. B
   18. A
   19. C
   20. B

SUPPORTING DETAILS:
Review Test 1
1. details
2. main idea (*or* point)
3. map
4. B
5. A

SUPPORTING DETAILS:
Review Test 2
A.
Main idea: *People lie for five main reasons.*
1. To prevent discomfort
2. To avoid conflict
3. To be socially acceptable
4. To increase or decrease interaction with someone
5. To have greater control over a situation
B. 6. Five main reasons
7. Another
8. also
9. In addition
10. Finally

SUPPORTING DETAILS:
Review Test 3
A.
Main idea: *Colonial Americans experienced dangerous medical treatments.*

Bloodletting	Sweating	Purging

Forcing patients to swallow syrup that would make them vomit

B. 5. a number of dangerous medical treatments

Note: Wording of answers to the outlines and maps in these tests may vary.

SUPPORTING DETAILS:
Review Test 4
1. B 6. B
2. B 7. A
3. A 8. B
4. D 9. B
5. D 10. A

SUPPORTING DETAILS:
Mastery Test 1
A. 1. Write often.
2. Organize your material with an outline.
3. Write in a plain style.
4. Tighten your writing.
5. First of all
6. Also
B.
Main idea: *Here are candidates for the lowest circles of Hell.*

Child molesters	Selfish politicians	Terrorists

10. Next, Last

SUPPORTING DETAILS:
Mastery Test 2
A. 1. Drug abuser cannot stop using or drinking.
2. Drug abuser turns into a "different" person when using.
3. User makes excuses for using drugs.
4. User will try to cover up drug use or will pretend it isn't that bad.
5. Abuser will forget what happens while he or she is high or drunk.
6. Abuser will be the last to recognize he or she has a problem.
B.
Main idea: *Several theories explain why people yawn.*

Boosts oxygen level in blood	Helps body change its level of alertness	Gives the body exercise

10. Any two of the following: One, second, another

SUPPORTING DETAILS:
Mastery Test 3
A. 1. Don't trust appearances.
  a. A dog wagging its tail isn't always friendly.
2. Be cautious.
  a. Let a dog see and sniff you before petting it.
3. Watch for warning signs.
  a. Dogs that stare with lowered heads are probably not friendly.
B.
Main idea: *Here are steps for effective written complaints.*

Address complaint to person in charge.	Write complaint in a clear, matter-of-fact way.	Explain exactly what action you want taken.

10. First, Next, Finally

SUPPORTING DETAILS:
Mastery Test 4

A. 1. Uniforms would save money for parents and children.
   b. They wouldn't have to buy designer jeans, fancy sneakers, and other high-priced clothing.
2. Students would not have to spend time worrying about clothes.
   b. They could concentrate on schoolwork and learning, not on making a fashion statement.
3. Uniforms would help all students get along better.
   b. Students from modest backgrounds would not have to feel inferior because of lower-cost clothes.

B.
Main idea: *A number of factors influence the pace of aging.*

Genes   Lifestyle   Social forces

Older people who are lonely often age faster than those who are involved with others.

SUPPORTING DETAILS:
Mastery Test 5

A. 1. Temperature
   a. If a workspace is too warm, workers become cranky and uncomfortable.
2. Color
   b. Blue soothes workers.
3. Lighting
   a. Bright, direct light encourages good listening, close concentration, and comfortable reading.

B.
Main idea: *Strategies can help heal family feuds.*

Get people to share the blame   Increase communication   Set realistic goals

Write notes, make phone calls, attend family events.

SUPPORTING DETAILS:
Mastery Test 6

A. 1. Through the eyes
   a. By glaring, people can show they are angry without saying a word.
2. Through facial expressions
   b. By looking at a face, one can tell if a person is sad, happy, afraid, or surprised.
3. Through body posture
   a. A person who is sitting upright or leaning forward shows great interest and attention.

B.
Main idea: *There are reasons that gemstones have high value.*

Beauty   Ability to resist damage   Scarcity

The most high-priced gems are very difficult and expensive to find.

Note: Wording of answers to the outlines and maps in these tests may vary.

13

LOCATIONS OF MAIN IDEAS:
Review Test 1

1. first
2. main idea
3. end
4. List
5. details

LOCATIONS OF MAIN IDEAS:
Review Test 2

1. Sentence 1
2. Sentence 5
3. Sentence 2
4. Sentence 1

LOCATIONS OF MAIN IDEAS:
Review Test 3

1. Sentence 2
2. Sentence 1
3. Sentence 1
4. Sentence 9

LOCATIONS OF MAIN IDEAS:
Review Test 4

1. B
2. B
3. D
4. D
5. A
6. A
7. D
8. B
9. A
10. D

LOCATIONS OF MAIN IDEAS:
Mastery Test 1

1. Sentence 5
2. Sentence 2
3. Sentence 1
4. Sentence 2
5. Sentence 1

LOCATIONS OF MAIN IDEAS:
Mastery Test 2

1. Sentence 1
2. Sentence 2
3. Sentence 6
4. Sentence 3
5. Sentence 1

LOCATIONS OF MAIN IDEAS:
Mastery Test 3

1. Sentence 2
2. Sentence 1
3. Sentence 5
4. Sentence 2
5. Sentence 1

LOCATIONS OF MAIN IDEAS:
Mastery Test 4

1. Sentence 6
2. Sentence 5
3. Sentence 2
4. Sentence 2
5. Sentence 1

LOCATIONS OF MAIN IDEAS:
Mastery Test 5

1. Sentence 6
2. Sentence 3
3. Sentence 3
4. Sentence 1
5. Sentence 9

LOCATIONS OF MAIN IDEAS:
Mastery Test 6

1. Sentence 2
2. Sentence 1
3. Sentence 7
4. Sentence 3
5. Sentence 2

RELATIONSHIPS I:
Review Test 1

1. Transitions
2. organization
3. addition
4. time
5. main idea

RELATIONSHIPS I:
Review Test 2

A. 1. C Before
2. B Another
3. E Then
4. A also
5. D First

B. 6. As
7. then
8. After (or When)
9. When (or After)
10. B

RELATIONSHIPS I:
Review Test 3

A. 1. One
2. Another
3. In addition
4. often
5. then

B. 6. B
7. A
8. B
9. B
10. A

RELATIONSHIPS I:
Review Test 4

1. D
2. B
3. B
4. A
5. C

6. F
7. B
8. also
9. A
10. C

RELATIONSHIPS I:
Mastery Test 1

A. 1. C In addition
2. E then
3. A Another
4. B Before
5. D One

B. 6. When
7. After
8. then
9. Before
10. B

RELATIONSHIPS I:
Mastery Test 2

A. 1. A also
2. E second
3. D During
4. C before
5. B Another

B. 6. First of all
7. Secondly
8. Moreover
9. Finally
10. A

RELATIONSHIPS I:
Mastery Test 3

A. 1–4. 3, 4, 2, 1
5. A

B. 6. B

C. 7. When
8. After
9. then
10. B

RELATIONSHIPS I:
Mastery Test 4

A. 1–4. 4, 1, 3, 2
5. B

B. 6. A

C. 7. later
8. When
9. then
10. Now

RELATIONSHIPS I:
Mastery Test 5

A. 1. A
2–3. *Any two of the following:* First of all, second, Last

B. 4. B
5–6. *Any two of the following:* In 1814, when, Then, In a short time, While, Three years later

C. 7. A
8. One
9. Another
10. third

RELATIONSHIPS I:
Mastery Test 6

A. 1. B
2–3. *Any two of the following:* earliest, in 540 B.C., then, until 1456, After, By the 1800s, in 1852, next, in the 1980s, today

B. 4. A
5–6. *Any two of the following:* First of all, Second, Also, final

C. 7. A
8–10.
Main idea: *For several reasons, some people find it hard to give appreciation or praise.*

| Received little praise or appreciation themselves | Insecurity | Fear |

15

RELATIONSHIPS II:
Review Test 1

1. C   4. A
2. B   5. C
3. C

RELATIONSHIPS II:
Review Test 2

A. 1. C like   **B.** 6. B
    2. E Therefore   7. A
    3. A For example   8. C
    4. D such as   9. A
    5. B in contrast   10. C

RELATIONSHIPS II:
Review Test 3

A. 1. C
    2. differently *or* In contrast
B. 3. B
    4. leading to *or* caused *or* As a result
       or led to
C. 5. A
    6. example
D. 7. B
    8. On the other hand *or* while *or*
       as opposed to
E. 9. C
    10. effects *or* cause *or* effect

RELATIONSHIPS II:
Review Test 4

1. A   6. A
2. C   7. D
3. C   8. C
4. A   9. A
5. C   10. C

RELATIONSHIPS II:
Mastery Test 1

A. 1. C For example   **B.** 6. B
    2. A As a result   7. C
    3. E just as   8. A
    4. D however   9. C
    5. B Because   10. B

RELATIONSHIPS II:
Mastery Test 2

A. 1. A explanation   **B.** 6. B
    2. B For instance   7. C
    3. E Therefore   8. B
    4. C However   9. C
    5. D same   10. A

RELATIONSHIPS II:
Mastery Test 3

A. 1–4. 3, 2, 1, 4
    5. C
B. 6. A
    7. For instance
C. 8. B
    9–10. *Any two of the following:* result,
          reasons, cause, reason, As a
          result, caused, Therefore

RELATIONSHIPS II:
Mastery Test 4

A. 1–4. 2, 3, 1, 4
    5. D
B. 6. B
    7. effects *or* As a result *or* effect
       or led to
C. 8. C
    9. In contrast *or* while *or* However
    10. In contrast *or* while *or* However

RELATIONSHIPS II:
Mastery Test 5

A. 1–4. 4, 3, 1, 2
    5. D
B. 6. B
    7. led to *or* affected by *or* result
C. 8. C
    9–10. *Any two of the following:*
          Unlike, Instead, Although,
          opposite, differ

RELATIONSHIPS II:
Mastery Test 6

A. 1. B
    2–5. 1. Managers who lack enough
            knowledge or experience
         2. Neglect
         3. Poor record-keeping
         4. Lack of money
B. 6. D
    7–10. Cold   Flu
           2. Headaches   1. Fever is
              may or may   typical.
              not occur.   2. Headaches
                              are likely.
                           4. Victims
                              may suffer
                              extreme
                              fatigue.

RELATIONSHIPS I and II:
Mastery Test 1

A. 1. A Because
    2. C In addition
    3. B For example
    4. E On the other hand
    5. D just like
B. 6. C However
    7. D such as
    8. B Before
    9. E Then
    10. A Another

RELATIONSHIPS I and II:
Mastery Test 2

A. 1. C
    2. When *or* later *or* after *or* then
B. 3. B
    4. like *or* Similarly *or* just as *or* alike
C. 5. A
    6. effects *or* led to
D. 7. A
    8. First *or* Another *or* third
E. 9. B
    10. reasons *or* reason *or* cause

INFERENCES:
Review Test 1

1. inferences   4. useful
2. context   5. useful
3. stated

INFERENCES:
Review Test 2

A. 2, 4
B. 3. B
   4. A
   5. B

INFERENCES:
Review Test 3

A. 1
B. 3, 5
C 3, 4

INFERENCES:
Review Test 4

1. B   6. D
2. A   7. D
3. B   8. A
4. C   9. B
5. B   10. D

INFERENCES:
Mastery Test 1

A. 1, 4, 5, 7
B. 5–6. B, C
   7–8. A, D
   9–10. B, C

INFERENCES:
Mastery Test 2

A. 2, 3, 6, 8
B. 5–6. B, D
   7–8. B, C
   9–10. A, D

INFERENCES:
Mastery Test 3

A. 1–2. B, D
   3–4. B, D
B. 5–7. A, C, E
   8–10. B, C, D

INFERENCES:
Mastery Test 4

A. 1–2. A, C
   3–4. A, D
B. 5–7. B, C, E
   8–10. B, C, E

INFERENCES:
Mastery Test 5

A. 1. C
   2. A
   3. C
B. 1, 3, 6, 7, 8

INFERENCES:
Mastery Test 6

A. 1, 4, 6, 7
B. 3, 4, 5, 8

IMPLIED MAIN IDEAS:
Review Test 1

1. implied
2. supporting details
3. narrow
4. broad
5. is bad (*or* is not worth seeing)

IMPLIED MAIN IDEAS:
Review Test 2

A. 1. Don't drive too fast (*or* Drive carefully)
2. A
3. B
B. 4. Books (*or* Novels)
5. Definitions

IMPLIED MAIN IDEAS:
Review Test 3

A. 1. D
2. C
3. B
B. 4. D
5. B

IMPLIED MAIN IDEAS:
Review Test 4

1. D
2. C
3. A
4. B
5. A
6. C
7. C
8. C
9. B
10. B

IMPLIED MAIN IDEAS:
Mastery Test 1

A. 1. C
B. 2. B
3. B
4. C
5. A
6. B
7. C
8. C
9. B
10. A

IMPLIED MAIN IDEAS:
Mastery Test 2

1. Tools
2. Sports (*or* Team sports *or* Professional sports)
3. Cookies
4. Workers
5. Crimes
6. Music (*or* Types of music)
7. Breakfast foods
8. Good working conditions
9. Wedding preparations
10. Ways to fail a course

IMPLIED MAIN IDEAS:
Mastery Test 3

1. C
2. B
3. C
4. D
5. A

IMPLIED MAIN IDEAS:
Mastery Test 4

1. A
2. D
3. B
4. B
5. B

IMPLIED MAIN IDEAS:
Mastery Test 5

1. C
2. A
3. B
4. A
5. C

IMPLIED MAIN IDEAS:
Mastery Test 6

1. D
2. B
3. D
4. A
5. C

THE BASICS OF ARGUMENT:
Review Test 1

1. general idea
2. support
3–5. point
    support
    support

THE BASICS OF ARGUMENT:
Review Test 2

A. 1. D

B.

Group 1	Group 2
A. P	A. S
B. S	B. S
C. S	C. P
D. S	D. S

C. 10. A

THE BASICS OF ARGUMENT:
Review Test 3

A.
- A. S
- B. S
- C. P
- D. S

B. 5–7. A, D, E
    8–10. A, C, E

THE BASICS OF ARGUMENT:
Review Test 4

1. D	6. D
2. B	7. D
3. A	8. B
4. D	9. D
5. D	10. C

THE BASICS OF ARGUMENT:
Mastery Test 1

A.

Group 1	Group 2
A. S	A. S
B. S	B. S
C. S	C. P
D. P	D. S

B. 9. B
C. 10. C

THE BASICS OF ARGUMENT:
Mastery Test 2

A. 1–3. B, C, D
    4–6. B, C, E
    7–9. B, C, D

B. 10. C

THE BASICS OF ARGUMENT:
Mastery Test 3

A.

Group 1	Group 2
A. S	A. P
B. S	B. S
C. P	C. S
D. S	D. S

B. 9. C
C. 10. B

THE BASICS OF ARGUMENT:
Mastery Test 4

A. 1–3. A, B, D
    4–6. A, B, D
    7–9. A, B, E

B. 10. C

THE BASICS OF ARGUMENT:
Mastery Test 5

A.
- A. S
- B. S
- C. P
- D. S

B. 5–7. A, B, E
C. 8. B
    9. A
    10. B

THE BASICS OF ARGUMENT:
Mastery Test 6

A.
- A. S
- B. P
- C. S
- D. S

B. 5–7. B, C, E
C. 8. (Group 1) B
    9. (Group 2) B
    10. (Group 3) C

Answers to the Reading Selections in Part II

1 WINNERS, LOSERS, OR JUST KIDS?

Vocabulary Questions

1. B	6. B flaunted
2. C	7. D morose
3. C	8. A endeared
4. D	9. E sheepish
5. A	10. C metamorphosis

Comprehension Questions

1. D	6. D
2. A	7. B
3. B	8. D
4. C	9. A
5. B	10. C

Summarizing

1. C
2. C
3. A

4 READ ALL ABOUT IT

Vocabulary Questions

1. A	6. A chaos
2. D	7. D stunned
3. C	8. C landmark
4. B	9. E unique
5. B	10. B decipher

Comprehension Questions

1. B	6. B
2. D	7. B
3. A	8. C
4. C	9. T
5. B	10. B

Summarizing *(Note: Wording of answers may vary.)*

1. distributing mail in a bank.
2. DeBlasio was offered a promotion.
3. a reading group
4. her friends about the problem she had with reading.

2 THE STORYTELLER

Vocabulary Questions

1. B	6. D reluctant
2. B	7. E scowl
3. A	8. A inappropriate
4. B	9. B lame
5. C	10. C prowling

Comprehension Questions

1. C	6. B
2. D	7. B
3. D	8. A
4. A	9. B
5. C	10. D

Outlining

2. The children begin to misbehave.
5. The aunt challenges the bachelor to tell a story.
6. The bachelor's story is about a good little girl who is eaten by a wolf.
8. The aunt is horrified by the bachelor's story.

5 ADULT CHILDREN AT HOME

Vocabulary Questions

1. C	6. C phenomenon
2. B	7. B fixed
3. A	8. E ruefully
4. D	9. D precautions
5. A	10. A consent

Comprehension Questions

1. C	6. D
2. A	7. A
3. A	8. C
4. D	9. C
5. F	10. T

Outlining

3. B
4. A
5. D
6. C

3 DISASTER AND FRIENDSHIP

Vocabulary Questions

1. B	6. E stereotyped
2. C	7. B intensified
3. C	8. C related
4. A	9. A bearing
5. C	10. D severely

Comprehension Questions

1. B	7. C
2. A	8. A
3. D	9. B
4. B	10. D
5. C	
6. *Any two of the following:* When, after, eventually	

Mapping

B —> F —> E —> D —> C —> A

6 HOW TO MAKE IT IN COLLEGE

Vocabulary Questions

1. B	6. E relatively
2. A	7. C hurdle
3. A	8. A distracted
4. C	9. D maintain
5. B	10. B hermit

Comprehension Questions

1. B	6. A
2. C	7. B
3. C	8. T
4. C	9. D
5. D	10. A

Outlining *(Note: Wording of answers may vary.)*

Central point: There are practical steps you can take to make yourself successful in college.

A2. Get into a study frame of mind.
A6. Review your textbook and your notes.
B2. Make up a study schedule.
B3. Use "to-do" lists.
C3. If your problems are overwhelming, see a counselor.

7 FALSE IDEAS ABOUT READING

Vocabulary Questions		Comprehension Questions	
1. B	6. B dry	1. B	6. C
2. C	7. C passive	2. D	7. B
3. A	8. E sound	3. B	8. D
4. B	9. D resources	4. B	9. D
5. D	10. A asserted	5. D	10. T

Outlining *(Note: Wording of answers may vary.)*
Central point: Three myths about reading keep people from
becoming better readers.
   1. The first myth is that every word must be read.
   2. The second myth is that reading once is enough.
   3. The third myth is that reading has to be work.

9 DEALING WITH FEELINGS

Vocabulary Questions		Comprehension Questions	
1. B	6. D perceived	1. B	7. for instance,
2. D	7. E seethe	2. D	example
3. C	8. A decipher	3. A	8. C
4. A	9. C inconsequential	4. A	9. B
5. B	10. B elated	5. C	10. C
		6. C	

Mapping *(Note: Wording of answers may vary.)*
Central point: There are three ways that people deal with
their feelings; while each is appropriate at times, the last
one is especially useful for educating others about how you
want them to treat you.

Withholding feelings	Displaying feelings	Describing feelings
means keeping them inside.	*means* expressing them through a nonverbal or verbal reaction.	*means* putting them into words.

8 ARE YOU A GOOD LISTENER?

Vocabulary Questions		Comprehension Questions	
1. C	6. D prone	1. A	7. *Any two of*
2. A	7. E prospects	2. C	*the following:*
3. B	8. C distraction	3. C	example,
4. D	9. B demeanor	4. A	for example,
5. C	10. A curb	5. F	to illustrate,
		6. First,	such as
		Also 8. T	
		9. B	
		10. C	

Mapping *(Note: Wording of answers may vary.)*
Rule 1: Look at the other person.   *Rule 2:* Ask questions.

Central point: Following six basic guidelines can help you
become a better listener.

Rule 4: Don't change the subject.   *Rule 6:* Be responsive.

10 CHILDHOOD STRESS AND RESILIENCE

Vocabulary Questions		Comprehension Questions	
1. B	6. A adverse	1. C	6. B
2. D	7. C console	2. A	7. D
3. C	8. B compensate	3. A	8. A
4. D	9. D resilience	4. B	9. D
5. C	10. E subject	5. C	10. B

Summarizing *(Note: Wording of answers may vary.)*
   1. divorce or death of parents, hospitalization, poverty,
      wars, earthquake, homelessness, and violence
   2. psychological
   3. resilient children.
   4. family, learning experiences, reduced risk, and
      compensating experiences.

Answers to the Combined-Skills Tests in Part III

COMBINED SKILLS:
Mastery Test 1

1. D	5. D
2. C	6. B
3. A	7. B
4. B	8. A

COMBINED SKILLS:
Mastery Test 2

1. A	5. D
2. A	6. A
3. C	7. A
4. B	8. D

COMBINED SKILLS:
Mastery Test 3

1. A	5. D
2. D	6. B
3. A	7. D
4. D	8. B

COMBINED SKILLS:
Mastery Test 4

1. A	5. C
2. B	6. A
3. A	7. B
4. C	8. B

COMBINED SKILLS:
Mastery Test 5

1. D	5. B
2. B	6. D
3. B	7. B
4. D	8. C

COMBINED SKILLS:
Mastery Test 6

1. B	5. A
2. D	6. D
3. D	7. A
4. C	8. A

COMBINED SKILLS:
Mastery Test 7

1. A	5. B
2. C	6. C
3. A	7. B
4. A	8. D

COMBINED SKILLS:
Mastery Test 8

1. D	5. D
2. C	6. C
3. C	7. B
4. B	8. A

COMBINED SKILLS:
Mastery Test 9

1. B	5. B
2. A	6. B
3. B	7. C
4. D	8. D

COMBINED SKILLS:
Mastery Test 10

1. D	5. C
2. A	6. C
3. B	7. B
4. C	8. D

COMBINED SKILLS:
Mastery Test 11

1. C	5. B
2. C	6. D
3. A	7. A
4. B	8. C

COMBINED SKILLS:
Mastery Test 12

1. C	5. C
2. C	6. B
3. B	7. D
4. A	8. D

COMBINED SKILLS:
Mastery Test 13

1. B	5. B
2. D	6. A
3. C	7. B
4. B	8. C

COMBINED SKILLS:
Mastery Test 14

1. B	5. B
2. D	6. D
3. C	7. C
4. C	8. D

COMBINED SKILLS:
Mastery Test 15

1. C	5. C
2. A	6. C
3. C	7. D
4. D	8. C

SUGGESTED ANSWERS TO THE DISCUSSION QUESTIONS IN PART I

Note: The numbers in parentheses refer to paragraphs in the reading. Also, for some questions, additional related questions have been included to enhance class discussion.

1 RESPONSIBILITY, M. Scott Peck

1. *Peck says that some people will go to ridiculous lengths to avoid assuming responsibility for their personal problems. What is ridiculous about the sergeant's behavior? About the young wife's behavior?*

    Both the sergeant and the young wife go to absurd lengths to justify their behavior. The sergeant invents numerous excuses for not pursuing activities other than drinking, even activities that he claims to enjoy. He then claims that it's the lack of pleasurable activities that drive him to drink. The young wife would rather complain and even attempt suicide (weakly) than make the small effort of learning to drive a stick shift.

    What might the sergeant and the young wife have done if they had assumed responsibility for their problems?

2. *What details might Peck have included in this selection if he had chosen students as examples? What responsibilities do students typically avoid? What excuses do they make?*

    Students frequently fail to take responsibility for their academic performance. Rather than do what is necessary to do well in class, they blame other people and circumstances for their own choices: "My best friend moved, and I had to help him," "I didn't study because I forgot to take my book home," "I didn't know there was a test," "I had to go to a party, so I didn't have time to write my paper."

3. *Peck writes that "we must accept responsibility for a problem before we can solve it." What does he mean by that? Do you agree? Use examples from your own life or someone else's to support your view.*

    Peck means that ultimately, the only person with power over an individual's problems is that individual. If we fool ourselves into believing that our problem is not our own responsibility, then we can allow ourselves to avoid taking responsibility. Only when we say, "This is my problem—not someone else's," can we begin to solve the problem. Students' opinions of Peck's statement will vary. Their personal examples will give them a chance to consider what taking personal responsibility for one's problems means.

4. *Why do you think it's so difficult for people to take responsibility for their problems?*

    Answers will vary. Reasons for people's reluctance to take responsibility include the following:

    - Laziness—it's just easier not to
    - Fear—a person may be afraid of taking responsibility and then failing or being in an new, unfamiliar situation
    - The lure of gaining sympathy from others by complaining about a situation, rather than trying to fix it.

2 ALL THE GOOD THINGS, Sister Helen P. Mrosla

1. *In this story, we read of two classroom incidents involving Sister Helen and her students. In one, she briefly taped a third-grader's mouth closed. In another, she encouraged junior-high students to think of things they liked about one another. In your opinion, what do these two incidents tell about Sister Helen? What kind of teacher was she? What kind of person?*

Both classroom incidents reveal Sister Helen as a sincere, well-meaning teacher. In the first incident, she is inexperienced; by the time of the second incident, she has become a skilled teacher with excellent judgment. In telling about the first classroom incident, Sister Helen shows her objectivity and lack of pride by saying of herself, "I made a novice teacher's mistake" (3). Her action in taping Mark's mouth shut seems to embarrass her, but she feels she has to carry through on her promise. The second classroom incident involves a mature teacher who is able to judge her students' mood and instinctively react in a way that would accomplish her purpose, and more. Her decision to have the students write down nice things about one another demonstrates her desire to see her students enjoy school and appreciate one another, not merely learn their academic subjects.

2. *Why do you think so many of Sister Helen's students kept their lists for so long? Why were the lists so important to them? What souvenir of the past have you kept for a long time? What does it mean to you?*

Students probably kept the lists because they represented something very positive. The lists were concrete evidence of qualities others liked about them, something they might otherwise have never, or rarely, encountered. The lists could be read again and again through the years. People rarely have a chance to experience praise in such a lasting, concrete form. Students' answers about souvenirs they treasure will reveal things that are important to them.

Do you remember something positive that was said about you years ago? How important was that comment to your self-image?

3. *At the end of the story, Sister Helen tells us that she "cried for Mark and for all his friends who would never see him again." Do you think she might have been crying for other reasons, too? Explain what they might be.*

Sister Helen might also have been moved by the realizations that her assignment had been so valued and that her students had been in such need of appreciation.

4. *"All the Good Things" has literally traveled around the world. Not only has it been reprinted in numerous publications, but many readers have sent it out over the Internet for others to read. Why do you think so many people love this story? Why do they want to share it with others?*

The story reminds readers of how much we all want and need the affirmation of others. Some people who read it are probably moved to get in touch with loved ones and let them know that they are appreciated. The sharing of Sister Helen's story may be an indirect way of reminding others to tell friends and relatives, especially young people, their good points.

3 GROUP PRESSURE, Rodney Stark

1. *Were you at all surprised by the results of Solomon Asch's experiment? If you had been one of the subjects, do you think you would have stuck to your answers, or would you have gone along with the group? Why?*

Students are likely to express surprise at the large number (75 percent) of subjects who eventually went along with the erroneous conclusions, at least some of the time. Some will probably insist they would never bow to group pressure and deny the evidence of their own eyes. Others may be sympathetic to the idea that it would be difficult to resist the temptation to fit in with the group by seeming to agree with the others' conclusions.

2. *What reasons might the subjects in the Asch experiment have had for eventually giving in and accepting the group's wrong answers?*

Answers will vary. Some subjects might have begun to doubt their own judgment or thought they'd misunderstood the instructions. Others might have reacted to the feeling that they were being tricked or that they would mess up the experiment in some way if they insisted on giving an answer contrary to the others.

What characteristic or characteristics do you think are responsible for "the behavior of those who steadfastly refused to accept the group's misjudgments" (9)?

3. *Stark refers to the Asch experiment as a "weak group situation," one in which the group is made up of strangers and the stakes are not very high. What might a "strong group situation" be? Give examples.*

If a weak group situation includes strangers and relatively unimportant stakes, a strong group situation would involve acquaintances or even more closely-related people and more important consequences. An example of a strong group situation might be a boy whose family and friends strongly oppose his dating a girl of another race or religion. The group would be made up of people he's strongly influenced by, and the stakes (the possible loss of their support and friendship) would be high. Other examples: a gang pressuring a member to commit an illegal act, and a group of students expecting a friend to help them make fun of another student who is perceived as different.

4. *Have you ever been in a situation when you wanted to resist group pressure? What was the situation, and why did you want to resist? What could you have done to resist?*

Answers will vary. Most people have faced situations where they felt torn between their individual desires and the desires of a group.

4 TOUCH SPARKS LOVE, Phyllis Spangler

1. *Why do you think parental touch was such a good solution for Debbie's problem? Did touch play a positive role in your childhood, or was there a lack of touching? If you have children, how do you use touch to show them your love?*

Parental touch was important to Debbie because it was a tangible expression of love. Although she had learned to "tune out" her parents' words, she could not ignore their affectionate touch. It was a good solution too because it was something her parents could do any time they were with Debbie. It was a silent but persuasive way of constantly saying, "We love you."

2. *Can you think of any other ways that busy parents, perhaps with several children, can give loving attention to all their children? Describe your ideas.*

Answers will vary; there are many ways that busy parents can show that they love and value their children, including the following:
- Display children's artwork or writing on the refrigerator.
- Make a point of saying goodnight to each child, spending a few quiet moments with each at bedtime.
- Schedule a special time to be alone with each child regularly—perhaps taking one child out for breakfast once a week.
- Plan family activities that will appeal to everyone, such as making popcorn and watching a video together or reading aloud.
- Notice and encourage each child's special talents.

3. *The author mentions that it took her and her husband a long time to admit that they needed help for their family. Why do you think it took so long? Why would it be difficult for parents to admit that they need professional help for their children? Explain.*

Parents probably find it difficult to ask for professional help with their children because they are afraid that they will be shown to be bad or inadequate parents. They are embarrassed not to have all the answers. They may look back at their own parents and think, "They managed without help, and I should be able to, too." Also, they may be afraid that getting professional help will reveal even worse problems than they already know about.

4. *Spangler at first did not want to go to the mental health center to get help for her daughter because she feared being seen there. Have you ever found yourself in a similar position—where you wanted to do something positive but you were too afraid of what others might think? For instance, you may have wanted to get tutoring or counseling for yourself. Tell about your experience.*

Answers will vary.

5 BODY LANGUAGE, Beth Johnson

1. *How aware of body language were you before you read this article? After reading it, might you behave any differently in situations where you are meeting people for the first time? Explain.*

   Students will realize that they can get a sense of someone they meet not just through what the person says, but by his or her body language. Examples will vary.

   Students might enjoy choosing one environment in which to note body language for a few moments and then reporting on their observations the next day.

2. *What is some of the "vocabulary" of classroom body language? Consider both students' and teachers' nonverbal communication.*

   Some common classroom body language includes the teacher's expression of authority by standing over a sitting student, or his or her crouching down to a student's level when trying to establish a closer connection. An instructor may stop and stare hard at a misbehaving student to demand his or her attention. Students show they are bored, attentive, distracted, or annoyed by such nonverbal actions as slumping in their seats with their eyes closed, sitting up straight and making eye contact with the instructor, playing with a pencil, or rolling their eyes and shifting position.

3. *Johnson gives several examples of ritual and body language in courtship. What others could you add?*

   Answers will vary. In seeking answers to this question, students can think of recent social scenes and personal relationships.

4. *Johnson writes, "Body language can be explained only within its context. . . . you shouldn't expect to find a 'dictionary' for reliable definitions of . . . tapping toes." Give some examples in which certain body language has different meanings in different situations. For example, what are some different meanings that tapping toes might have?*

   The interpretation of body language depends very much on the context in which it occurs. For instance, tapping one's toes could mean that one was impatient, or nervous, or that one was keeping time with some real or imaginary music. Or one person touching another's hand during a conversation could be a gesture of sympathy or of romantic interest, or it could be a way of emphasizing a point.

6 BEHIND CLOSED DOORS: VIOLENCE IN THE FAMILY, Michael S. Bassis, Richard J. Gelles, and Ann Levine

1. *Why do you think the researchers "asked a representative sample of Americans how they resolved family conflicts" instead of using official statistics such as police reports? What did their method accomplish that relying on official statistics would not have accomplished?*

Official statistics reflect only the small percentage of violent incidents that are actually reported to police. Asking a representative sample of families gives a much broader picture of the violence that is a daily occurrence in many homes.

2. *What myths about family violence did the survey disprove? Why might these myths have existed in the first place?*

The author lists three myths that were disproved: that violence among family members is rare (3); that family violence is primarily a problem of the poor and uneducated (3–4); and that people who abuse a loved one are mentally ill (5). These myths may have arisen out of people's need to idealize the family home as a safe, loving place and to convince themselves that they could not fall victim to family violence—that it's something that happens to "other" people.

3. *Were you or was someone you know ever punished with physical force as a child? If so, what do you think have been the effects of this use of force?*

Answers will vary.

4. *If people know that a neighbor is violent at home, what do you think they should do? What can society—for instance, schools, religious institutions, government, the media—do to prevent further violence in families?*

Answers will vary. Some options include reporting the neighbor to the police or other authorities, personally confronting the violent person, or trying to get someone whom the neighbor respects (a relative, friend, or member of the clergy) to talk to the abuser about getting help for his or her violent tendencies.

    The schools, media, churches, and other institutions could help by speaking out openly about how widespread family violence is. Many people involved in family violence decline to seek help because they think their family must be very unusual or abnormal, and they are embarrassed to admit the problem. Employers could offer counseling services as part of their employee benefit packages, so that workers who are under stress could deal with their problems, rather than take them out on their families.

7 THE MOST HATEFUL WORDS, Amy Tan

1. *In their discussion at the end of the essay, Tan chooses to keep her emotions hidden from her mother. Why do you think she does this?*

Amy knows that her mother, now elderly, is in fragile health, her mind impaired by Alzheimer's disease. Amy's tears would probably only confuse and upset her mother, who is already feeling worried about her memory of having hurt her daughter. Amy chooses to do the kinder thing, which is to comfort her mother and reassure her that everything is all right.

2. *Have you ever known someone who, because of Alzheimer's disease or a mental illness, did or said things that didn't make sense? How did you respond—in your thoughts or actions—to his or her confusion? Did you "play along" or try to show the person that he or she wasn't being rational?*

Answers will vary. In the case of persons with Alzheimer's disease, trying to insist that the person be rational would probably only worry and confuse him or her.

3. *Did you have a difficult relationship with one or both of your parents? Were the problems more the result of your teenage behavior or of their behavior? Looking back, what do you think one or both of you could have done to make the relationship better?*

Answers will vary. Older students may have more perspective than younger ones on the ways their own behavior contributed to a difficult situation.

4. *This essay makes the reader think of the phrase "forgive and forget." But is this advice always fair or realistic? Are there times when it is better to hold someone responsible for his or her actions than to forgive and forget? Explain.*

"Forgive and forget" may be good advice for occasions when someone has offended you without intending to or has done something uncharacteristically thoughtless. But if someone is habitually unkind, dishonest, or otherwise offensive, "forgive and forget" may be less appropriate. By saying, "No, I won't forgive and forget," you may cause a person to examine his or her own behavior and realize how it hurts other people. It is also possible to "forgive" without "forgetting"—that is, you may forgive someone for harming you, while you remember to protect yourself against that person harming you again in the future.

8   HALF A POUND OF HAM, Bernadete Piassa

1. *This brief essay reveals quite a bit about Piassa. What do we learn about what her life is like and what she is like?*

We learn the following about Piassa:

- She is a journalist and well-educated.
- She is the mother of three children.
- Piassa speaks three languages.
- She is concerned about what others think of her.
- In her own country, she thought of herself as a confident, strong person, while in the United States she is often shy and timid.
- Although she thinks of herself as somewhat cowardly, we also see her forcing herself to do courageous things, such as speak English in public.
- While she still does not feel at home in America, she no longer feels she quite belongs in her own country, either.

2. *Piassa writes, "I am so tired of explanations" (paragraph 9). What does she feel the need to explain? Why does she feel this need?*

The pressure for Piassa to explain herself comes from her sense that Americans view her, with her accent and less-than-perfect English, as inferior to them and bad for their country. She wants to prove to them that she, too, is a human being worthy of their respect and even friendship. Piassa feels she has to answer the "thousand questions floating in [people's] eyes" (9) to show that she "came from a good family and yes, your kids can play with mine without getting harmed, no, I am not going to eat you, yes, I speak three languages, I am not an illiterate, no, I don't intend to destroy America's values, yes, I would like to see your country in better shape, no, I am not going to steal Americans' jobs" (9).

3. *Piassa could have written in a general way about the many discouraging challenges that foreigners face in a new country. Why do you think she chose to write in a very specific way about one small everyday challenge?*

By focusing in detail on the small matter of buying ham at the supermarket, Piassa helps us clearly imagine the dozens of minor frustrations that daily face a person trying to adjust to a new language and culture.

4. *Have you ever been in a situation where you did not fit in? How did it make you feel, and how did you deal with the situation?*

Answers will vary.

9 LIGHTING A MATCH, Regina Ruiz

1. *During the years of her unhappy marriage, Ruiz told herself, "The children need me, and I cannot admit failure to my parents back in Venezuela." Do these seem to you like understandable reasons for remaining in an unhappy relationship? Are they* good *reasons?*

Most people find such reasons understandable. But one could argue that they are not good reasons since they don't address the problem of a very unhappy relationship. Children raised in an unhappy marriage may take that as their model for future relationships, believing that it is normal to be unhappy. And most family members or friends would ultimately rather see a person happy and fulfilled than living in a miserable situation.

2. *Ruiz writes that after she enrolled in college, she was proud of herself "for not falling into the garbage pit waiting so close by." What do you think she means by the words "the garbage pit waiting so close by"? Have you ever made a choice that you feel either saved you from or dropped you into "a garbage pit?"*

For Ruiz, "the garbage pit" probably meant a life of frustration and fear—i.e., the life she would have lived if she had not taken steps toward a better one. She could easily have been overwhelmed by her problems and gone through the rest of her life feeling she was a failure. Answers will vary concerning what students have seen as "the garbage pit" waiting for them— but they will reflect students' understanding of the results of bad decisions in challenging circumstances.

   Do you know someone, who like Ruiz, had to choose between accepting a bad situation or taking steps toward a better life? Tell about that person.

3. *Like Ruiz, adults who return to college often have a difficult time balancing the demands of their work, family, and classes. What challenges do you face as a student? What ways have you found to deal with them?*

Answers will vary.

4. *Ruiz briefly explains her decision to become a nurse. Why have you chosen your own course of study? What about it interests you? What do you hope it will offer to you after college?*

Answers will vary.

10 DO IT BETTER! Ben Carson, M.D., with Cecil Murphey

1. *Why did Bennie consider himself the "dumbest kid in class"? How did his image of himself affect his schoolwork?*

   He was a new student at his school and had gotten off to a poor start by giving frequent wrong answers in class. The other students had laughed at him and labeled him "dumb." Deciding that they were right, Ben made no effort to improve his grades and instead escaped into activities that he enjoyed: watching TV and playing outside.

2. *The author recalls his failure in the classroom as an eight-year-old child by writing, "Perhaps I wasn't emotionally able to learn much." Why does he make this statement? What things in a child's home or social life might interfere with his or her education?*

   Ben was distracted by his parents' marital troubles, their separation, and the disappearance of his father. Children whose lives outside of school are unsettled often find it hard to concentrate on schoolwork. Parents' problems, poverty, fighting, or substance abuse in the home are a few of the factors that could interfere with a child's readiness to learn.

3. *Part of Carson's mother's plan for helping her sons to improve their schoolwork was limiting their television watching to two programs a week. How much of a role do you think this limit played in the success of her plan? Do you agree with her that unrestricted television watching can be harmful to children?*

   It seems clear that restricting the boys' TV watching did benefit them. They used their former TV-watching time to read, study, and discover new interests. TV watching is a passive experience that does little to stimulate children's minds. Many parents, teachers, and other people in contact with children have observed a connection between heavy TV watching and poor school performance.

4. *Reading on a regular basis helped turn Carson's life around. Think about your daily schedule. If you were to do regular reading, where in your day could you find time to relax for half an hour and just read? What do you think would be the benefits of becoming a regular reader?*

   Answers will vary. Here are some of the benefits of being a regular reader:
   - The pleasure of losing oneself in a good story
   - The satisfaction of learning about someone or something one is interested in
   - Learning more about life and the world in general
   - Becoming an informed citizen
   - Improving one's vocabulary

SUGGESTED ANSWERS TO THE DISCUSSION QUESTIONS IN PART II

Note: The numbers in parentheses refer to paragraphs in the reading. Also, for some questions, additional related questions have been included to enhance class discussion.

1 WINNERS, LOSERS, OR JUST KIDS? Dan Wightman

1. *What does Wightman really mean by "winners" and "losers"? Why does the title also say, "or Just Kids"?*

   Wightman describes winners as people who succeeded academically, were attractive, and had money (1). He describes losers as those who did poorly in school (spending more time "tuning cars and drinking beer" than studying) and socially, and who enlisted in the Army instead of advancing their careers by going to a university (2). By adding "or Just Kids" to the title, Wightman suggests that "winners" and "losers" are not as fitting terms as they at first may seem to be.

2. *What do the first two paragraphs of this selection accomplish?*

   In addition to providing the definitions discussed in question 1, the first two paragraphs set the stage for the author's reunion experience and its answers to the questions "Did the 'winners' really win? Did the 'losers' really lose?"

3. *What is the meaning of the sentence "The past is fiction"? To what extent do you think it's true, if at all? In what ways isn't it true?*

   In writing "The past is fiction," Burroughs implies that the only important truth is what a person does from the present onward. That idea might be considered true to the extent that we overcome our pasts and build a good present and future. Yet it can be argued that there are many things in anyone's past that will always influence his or her future.

4. *Wightman writes that he "wondered why he was different, and had more luck, less guilt" than others. What factors do you suppose are involved in determining whether or not people shake their "loser's image"? What factors does Wightman name?*

   Wightman suggests that "more luck, less guilt" help a person lose a "loser's image"(13). He also suggests that not despairing, not regressing and not giving up (13) lead to success. What other factors might help someone overcome a slow start toward a successful life? Some factors to consider: goals, support, education, willpower, and the development of one's abilities.
   How might guilt keep someone from shedding a loser's image?

2   THE STORYTELLER, Saki

1. Why do you think the children so preferred the bachelor's story to the aunt's?

While the aunt's story was dull, predictable, and moralistic, the bachelor's story was full of colorful details and danger. Best of all, it had a surprising twist at the end, when the little girl was actually punished for being so good.

2. How do you tend to react when you see children misbehaving in public? Would you ever consider offering to help their parents by doing something like telling the children a story? Why do you think the bachelor in the story decided to tell the children a story?

Answers regarding the students' own actions will vary. The bachelor may have had several reasons for telling the children a story. He was annoyed by their noisy behavior on the train and wanted them to sit quietly. He may have felt sorry for them for having to listen to their aunt's boring story. And he may have wanted to teach the aunt a lesson about how to entertain children.

3. When you were little, who was your favorite storyteller? Was it an adult in your life such as a parent or teacher, or was it a friend of yours, or was it a TV personality? What stories do you remember him or her telling or reading?

Answers will vary.

4. Did your parents (or other adults in your life) ever hold up other children as examples to you? What qualities did they admire in the other children? How did you respond to being compared to other children?

Answers will vary, but most children resent being compared to others. A more useful tactic is for parents to notice the good points in their child whenever possible, pointing them out and praising them.

3 DISASTER AND FRIENDSHIP, Chuck Wilson

1. Wilson was worried that the sheriff would be just "like the stereotyped image of the white Southern country sheriff." What is that image?

A common stereotype of a white Southern country sheriff includes these characteristics:

- racist
- unjust to blacks
- unwilling to help blacks
- anxious to get the worst possible sentences for convicted blacks

2. Wilson asked the woman in charge at the Chester Chamber of Commerce to help him find a job. Instead, she arranged for him to get some money and his car so he could go on to Florida. Why might she have done that?

In writing that the woman "understood my situation" (11), Wilson implies that, among other things, she understood he was treated unfairly by some. If so, she may have wished to help counteract that unfair treatment.

What experiences have you had or heard of in which someone helped a perfect stranger?

3. Wilson's experience was notable partly because it showed how wrong stereotypes can be. What experiences have you had in which people did not fit their stereotypes?

Perhaps we have all been surprised by unexpected behavior that contradicted our preconceptions. Students' memories of such experiences can be jogged by mentioning various types of people we tend to put into boxes that they don't fit: teachers, used-car salesmen, clergypersons, police officers, and racial and ethnic groups of all kinds.

4. How do stereotypes influence our treatment of other people?

Here are some questions to consider in answering:

- Do people pick—or reject—others as friends because of their background, age, or sex rather than because of what they really are like?
- Are people more likely to vote for—or against—someone because of his or her age, sex, race, or ethnic background?
- Do people tend to think that the woman in an office is a secretary?

4 READ ALL ABOUT IT, Fran DeBlasio

1. *Do you know anybody who has trouble reading? How does that trouble affect his or her life?*

Answers may include the areas with which DeBlasio has had trouble, including progressing in school, finding jobs, getting a driver's license, and hiding the inability to read from others.

2. *Just how difficult is it to live in our society without being able to read? To get an idea of the answer to this question, think about your activities at home, shopping, in restaurants, and driving. How much of what you've done involves reading?*

Daily reading includes the following:

- newspapers
- street signs
- menus
- recipes
- phone books
- written words on television and in movies
- signs identifying bus and train routes
- store and restaurant signs
- clothing tags telling materials and garment care
- lists of ingredients on cans and boxes of food.

3. *DeBlasio gives a bleak picture of the schools she attended. In what ways were your own schools like, or unlike, hers? Why do you think her teachers behaved as they did?*

Students might consider the idea that all too often, teachers (like people in all jobs) go along with a system and avoid responsibility. In addition, they may choose the easy way out. Finally, teachers may fail to see a student's true problems or understand how to solve them.
How can students overcome the effects of a poor education?

4. *We tend to think that people don't learn important new skills as they get older, but DeBlasio's story contradicts that idea. Describe a person or persons you know who have been able to learn new skills as they get older.*

Answers will vary but can include anyone who has learned new work skills, hobbies, etc. Students may wish to also mention people in the public eye who learned new skills. Former President Reagan, for example, learned to be a politician after a career in acting, and sports figures often go on to new careers after their sports careers end.

5 ADULT CHILDREN AT HOME, Marilyn Mack

1. *Do you know any cases of nesting? Why did the children return home? How did it work out?*

   Answers will vary.
   Why do we assume that children should move out of their parents' homes at a certain age?

2. *Do you think today's young adult children are having a harder time financially than their parents' generation? Or is the "standard of living they hoped for" higher? Or both?*

   While students may not be able to speak for "today's young adult children" in general, they can discuss cases they know of, including their own. They might contrast their own standard of living with their parents' at their age. Factors to consider include where they live, how often they can afford to eat out and go to movies, and how much credit they use. They might also contrast their own economic goals with those of their parents.

3. *Mack mentions the "people who've gotten in over their heads with credit cards and utility bills." Why do you think people get into this situation?*

   Students may wish to discuss cases they know of or to speculate in general as to why people get heavily into debt.
   What can people do to avoid getting heavily into debt?

4. *Do you agree that adult children who return home, "regardless of their financial situation," should pay some room and board? If not, what financial situations should exclude adult children from paying room and board?*

   Students who feel all adult children ought to pay some room and board should present one or more reasons in support of their view. Those who disagree may wish to discuss not only the relevant financial situations but also the noneconomic ways in which adult children can contribute.

6 HOW TO MAKE IT IN COLLEGE, NOW THAT YOU'RE HERE,
Brian O'Keeney

1. *What would you say is the single biggest obstacle between you and better grades? Do you need to get organized? Do you exaggerate your personal problems? How might O'Keeney's article help you overcome this obstacle?*

    Common obstacles between students and better grades:
    - Procrastination
    - Demands of friends
    - A job
    - Family obligations.

    Answers will vary concerning how to deal with such obstacles.

2. *Do you make "to-do" lists? If not, do you think you should? What are three items that you would put on your "to-do" list for today?*

    Answers will vary.
       Why do you think that writing a "to-do" list can be so helpful?

3. *"Sometimes, you've just got to hang tough," O'Keeney tells us (paragraph 21). What does he mean? What are some techniques for hanging tough, instead of giving in, that have worked for you or for people you know?*

    "Hanging tough" means refusing to allow problems, no matter how real they are, to interfere with one's goals. A person who hangs tough knows that life's circumstances are sometimes difficult, but that an achiever keeps on going anyway. Techniques for hanging tough might include such things as scheduling a specific, limited time to deal with a problem, but then setting that problem aside when it's time for study. Another hang-tough technique might be to refuse to let anything short of serious illness make you miss a class—to promise yourself that no matter how upset or worried you are, you will not allow yourself to skip class.

4. *O'Keeney writes in paragraph 27, "Look at your priorities. You want a degree, or a certificate, or a career." What are your priorities? Explain the kind of life you hope to have and how college fits into those plans.*

    Answers will vary.

7   FALSE IDEAS ABOUT READING, Robert and Pam Winkler

1. *Which one of the myths about reading is most helpful for you to know about? How has this myth affected your reading and study habits?*

Writing the myths on the board ("You must read every word," "Reading once is enough," "Reading has to be work") may help students focus on which is most helpful for them to know about. In discussing the myths and their relationships to reading, students may wish to differentiate between reading for school and reading for pleasure.

2. *Give an example of someone you know who has been influenced by one of the myths about reading. What would you tell this person to change his or her attitude?*

Students might think of a younger sibling or a friend who would benefit from knowing about one of the myths in this reading.

Do you know of anyone who has another type of reading problem? How might that problem be solved?

3. *What do you think are the benefits and dangers of not reading every word?*

The benefits of not reading every word, according to the Winklers, are not spending time on reading that doesn't meet the purpose (3) and that doesn't interest you (5). The dangers of skimming too much are that readers may miss important points and the supporting details that make sense of main points.

4. *The Winklers write that books can "help people discover and explore parts of themselves that they may not know existed." What do they mean by this? Use examples, if possible, from one or more books you have read.*

To answer this question, students must focus on what they have learned about themselves from reading. Have they read a psychology text that helped to explain their feelings, reactions, and/or family situation? Have they read a short story or novel with a character that gave them insight into themselves? Or have they read a how-to publication that helped them realize they could accomplish something new?

What do you wish you knew? Where might you find that information in books?

8 ARE YOU A GOOD LISTENER? Robert L. Montgomery

1. *Which of Montgomery's six rules for better listening are most helpful for you personally to remember?*

   Listing the rules on the board will help students choose which is most helpful. Those rules are: 1) Look at the other person, 2) Ask questions, 3) Don't interrupt, 4) Don't change the subject, 5) Check your emotions, 6) Be a responsive listener. In answering this question, students might think about times they had trouble conversing, missed important information, or missed sales or other job-related achievements.

2. *Which trait of poor listeners bothers you most when you are speaking to others? Give examples.*

   Students might consider the following:

   • Do friends ever interrupt your stories about your problems with stories of their own problems?
   • Do your parents interrupt you to tell you what they think you should be doing?
   • Do teachers look out the window while you talk to them?

3. *In paragraph 10, Montgomery contrasts the "product-pusher" with the "counselor-type salesperson." What does he mean by each of those terms, and what are the differences between them? What experiences have you had with either of those types? If you've encountered them both, which do you prefer?*

   The term "product-pusher" implies a type of salesperson whose emphasis is solely on explaining the product to the customer. The "counselor-type salesperson," writes Montgomery, "asks questions first" to discover the prospect's "needs, problems or objectives" (10). In other words, the counselor-type salesperson is more likely to try to sell you something you need because he or she has taken the time to find out what you need.

   Students' experiences with salespeople may range from department store clerks to insurance salespeople. In trying to answer this question, students can analyze the various sales methods and classify them according to Montgomery's two ways of selling.

4. *Montgomery writes in paragraph 2, "Listening is essential to our personal, professional, social, and family success." In what specific ways might listening contribute to success in each of those areas of our life? Give examples for each.*

   Following are examples of ways in which listening might be helpful in the areas listed:

   • Listening to feedback from friends, family, teachers, and bosses can help us improve and advance ourselves.
   • Listening to bosses and coworkers helps us follow directions and understand our jobs better.
   • Listening to family and friends helps us know and support them better and strengthens those relationships.

9 DEALING WITH FEELINGS, Rudolph F. Verderber

1. What is the difference between describing feelings and displaying them? How might Doris describe her feelings to Candy after Candy says, "That first paragraph isn't very well written" (paragraph 2)?

Describing feelings means explaining what emotions one is feeling (8); in contrast, displaying feelings means responding to, or acting on, those feelings in some way (5). For example, take a man who has just won a lottery. First he jumps into the air and yells "Whoopee!"; then he says, "Boy, I'm feeling so happy and thrilled." First the man displayed his feelings, and then he described them.

If Doris were to describe her feelings to Candy, she might say, "I feel very nervous when you stand over me, watch me work, and criticize my report as I'm trying to get it into shape."

2. What do you think would be Verderber's advice on "little lies"? (See paragraph 13.)

Judging by paragraph 13 of the reading, Verderber would probably advise people to allow others to express how they feel without making them feel guilty. He implies that since we feel the way we do, we should be free to describe those feelings. What we do about them is another matter.

3. Why do you think Verderber emphasizes describing feelings over the other two methods of dealing with feelings?

Verderber writes, "Describing is often the best strategy for dealing with feelings, not only because it gives you the best chance for a positive outcome but also, as we said, because describing feelings teaches people how to treat you" (9). We can assume that he also feels describing feelings avoids the drawbacks of the other two methods. The drawbacks of withholding feelings are possible physical and psychological problems (3); the drawback of expressing or displaying negative feelings is that interpersonal problems are created (6).

4. What are some examples from your own experience of withholding, expressing or displaying, and describing feelings? How useful was each?

To find examples of the three methods of dealing with feelings in their own lives, students can look at their family life, friendships, jobs, and classes.

10 CHILDHOOD STRESS AND RESILIENCE, Diane E. Papalia and Sally Wendkos Olds

1. *How has childhood changed since you were young? How was your own childhood different from that of your parents? What was better about your childhood as compared with childhood today? Compared with your parents' childhood? What was worse?*

   In comparing their own childhoods to those of today's children and of their parents, students might consider the following: educational and work opportunities, expectations of children, family and community values, and the national and international situations.

2. *Do you recall any experiences that you found particularly stressful as a child? If so, how did you deal with them?*

   To jog students' memories for answers to this question, the class might take another look at the box in the reading on page 508, titled "What Children Are Afraid Of." What fears did students have in regard to their parents, school, and the world? What embarrassing experiences caused them anxiety?

3. *The author states that children today are forced to grow up too quickly. What are some of the things that you believe children need time to learn and experience as children?*

   To answer this question, students might think about the best of their own childhood experiences. What childhood experiences do they especially value? Also, the class might take another look at the factors that seem to contribute to resilience (9–13). We can conclude from the list that certain experiences and relationships are desirable in childhood.

4. *Sometimes a child's healthy development is hindered by the very people who are supposed to encourage it—the child's parents, relatives, or friends. What do you believe could be done to prevent child abuse (both physical and mental)? Why do you think child abuse is so common in the United States?*

   Students will use their personal knowledge to discuss these two questions. From their discussion, a list might be compiled of the factors present in cases of child abuse (alcoholism, coming from a home with child abuse, etc.). You might also list on the board specific solutions suggested by students. Some broad categories of solutions include community support programs, educational programs in schools, and educational programs in the media.

MODEL NOTES AND ADDITIONAL ACTIVITIES FOR "THREE ADDITIONAL READINGS"

Comments and Suggestions

- This section contains the following for each of the three additional reading selections on pages 561–567 of the text:

  1. An outlining or mapping activity.

  2. The completed outline or map of the reading. These outlines and maps can be copied and distributed for comparison purposes after students have completed the activity or taken their own notes.

  3. A short quiz on the reading, which can be copied and given after students have finished taking notes on the reading. The quizzes will demonstrate to students how much they have learned simply through good notetaking. (Answers to the three quizzes are on page 54.)

- The three readings can be assigned one at a time throughout the semester after students have worked through "Supporting Details," Chapter 4 in Part I, in which outlining and mapping are explained.

- I suggest assigning the readings in terms of level of difficulty. From easiest to hardest, I would sequence the readings as follows:

  Food Choices (easiest)
  Class Profiles
  Paraphrasing (hardest)

- Following are some notetaking guidelines you may wish to copy and pass out and/or briefly go over with students.

Some Notetaking Guidelines

- Before beginning to take notes, carefully read through and mark the material.

- Here's how to mark material: Circle definitions, set off examples with an *Ex,* and underline or bracket ideas that seem especially important. Use numbers (1, 2, 3 . . .) to mark off major items in a series.

- Then take notes by writing down each heading in turn and listing the important ideas that you find under that heading. Think carefully about each heading; it is often a key to main ideas and major details.

- Keep outlines simple. Often just one level of symbols (1, 2, 3 . . .) will do.

- Sometimes you may want two levels, and they can be labeled as follows:

  1.
     a.
     b.
  2.
     a.
     b.

MAPPING ACTIVITY: "CLASS PROFILES"

The Four Social Classes in the U.S.

	Members (% of population; financial and work characteristics)	Lifestyle characteristics
Upper class	3-5% of pop. and at least 25% of wealth Upper-upper: live on interest of inherited wealth; ex.: Rockefellers Lower-upper: _____ _____	Time, money to enjoy and collect art; live in exclusive areas and socialize w/each other; have great power and influence in gov't and business
Middle class	40-50% of population—not as wealthy as upper class, but not in manual jobs of lower class Upper-middle class: _____ _____ _____ Exs.: doctors, lawyers, executives Lower-middle class— _____ _____ _____ _____ _____	Own suburban home, live a comfortable life
Working class	_____ _____ Skilled workers—may make more money than lower-middle class workers Exs: construction workers, plumbers _____ _____ _____	(no details given in reading)
Lower class	15-20% of population—"the underclass" The chronically unemployed, welfare recipients, poor aged, skilled factory workers who became unskilled in electronically-run factories	_____ _____ _____

A MAP OF "CLASS PROFILES"

The Four Social Classes in the U.S.

	Members (% of population; financial and work characteristics)	Lifestyle characteristics
Upper class	3-5% of pop. and at least 25% of wealth Upper-upper: live on interest of inherited wealth; ex.: Rockefellers Lower-upper: had to work for their money	Time, money to enjoy and collect art; live in exclusive areas and socialize w/each other; have great power and influence in gov't and business
Middle class	40-50% of population—not as wealthy as upper class, but not in manual jobs of lower class Upper-middle class: more prestige, income, and education then lower-middle class. Exs.: doctors, lawyers, executives Lower-middle class—larger in size, more diverse in occupation than upper-middle class. Exs.: small-business owners, salespersons, teachers, secretaries	Own suburban home, live a comfortable life
Working class	30-40% of population; in manual job without prestige Skilled workers—may make more money than lower-middle class workers Exs: construction workers, plumbers Unskilled workers—"the working poor" Examples: migrant workers, janitors, dishwashers	(no details given in reading)
Lower class	15-20% of population—"the underclass" The chronically unemployed, welfare recipients, poor aged, skilled factory workers who became unskilled in electronically-run factories	Run-down housing, old clothes, cheap foods, poor medical care

A QUIZ ON "CLASS PROFILES"

Check what you've learned in taking notes on "Class Profiles" by filling in each blank with the letter of the matching description.

_____ Lower-upper class   A. Includes the "working poor"

_____ Upper-middle class   B. Marked by joblessness and poverty

_____ Lower-middle class   C. Very rich with self-earned money

_____ Working class   D. Includes teachers and salespersons

_____ Lower class   E. Made up of professional and business people with high income and education

OUTLINING ACTIVITY: "FOOD CHOICES"

Complete the following outline.

Reasons for food choices:

1. _____—people like certain flavors; genetics may be a factor.

2. _____—no decision to make; eat cereal in morning because always have.

3. _____—every country and region has its own typical foods.

4. Social interactions—eating is a way to be part of a group; for example, _____

_____

5. Availability, convenience, and economy—people eat foods that are accessible, quick, and easy and affordable to prepare

6. Positive and negative associations—positive example is _____

_____; negative example is food a child is made to eat as punishment.

7. _____—people may eat to relieve boredom, depression, or anxiety.

8. Values—food choices may reflect religious beliefs (no meat during Lent), political views (boycotting vegetables picked by migrant workers), or environmental concerns (vegetables grown by local farmers to save fuel costs).

9. _____—choosing foods based on whether they will improve or harm physical appearance.

10. Nutrition—choosing foods to benefit health; for example, _____

_____

AN OUTLINE OF "FOOD CHOICES"

Reasons for food choices:

1. Personal preferences—people like certain flavors; genetics may be a factor.

2. Habit—no decision to make; eat cereal in morning because always have.

3. Ethnic heritage or tradition—every country and region has its own typical foods.

4. Social interactions—eating is a way to be part of a group; for example, going out for pizza with friends.

5. Availability, convenience, and economy—people eat foods that are accessible, quick, and easy and affordable to prepare

6. Positive and negative associations—positive example is turkey at Thanksgiving; negative example is food a child is made to eat as punishment.

7. Emotional comfort—people may eat to relieve boredom, depression, or anxiety.

8. Values—food choices may reflect religious beliefs (no meat during Lent), political views (boycotting vegetables picked by migrant workers), or environmental concerns (vegetables grown by local farmers to save fuel costs).

9. Body image—choosing foods based on whether they will improve or harm physical appearance.

10. Nutrition—choosing foods to benefit health; for example, eating large salad along with slice of pizza.

A QUIZ ON "FOOD CHOICES"

Check what you've learned in taking notes on "Food Choices" by answering the following questions.

_____ 1. Which sentence expresses the main idea of the selection?
   A. In choosing which foods to eat, people should put nutrition needs ahead of personal preference.
   B. While people choose foods for a variety of reasons, nutrition awareness should play a role as well.
   C. Most people have various positive and negative associations with certain foods.

_____ 2. Overeating and obesity often result when people eat
   A. for emotional comfort.
   B. foods with negative associations.
   C. for body image.

_____ 3. Eating restaurant food
   A. is always unhealthy.
   B. is usually cheaper than eating homemade food.
   C. limits food choices.

_____ 4. People eat foods out of habit because familiar foods
   A. are nutritious.
   B. tend to be cheaper.
   C. require no decisions and are comforting.

_____ 5. People can find nutritious foods among
   A. many new foods.
   B. many ordinary foods.
   C. both of the above.

OUTLINING ACTIVITY: "PARAPHRASING"

Complete the following outline of the selection.

Paraphrasing is a way to make a message clear by putting your understanding of it into words.

Two types of paraphrases (which can be used separately or together):

1. Content paraphrase: summarizes the meaning of the words
2. Feelings paraphrase: _____

   _____

When to paraphrase:

1. When you need a better understanding of a message, in terms of content and/or feelings
2. _____.
3. When you think what was said is not what the person meant to say because of its controversial nature or the person's emotional strain
4. _____.
5. _____.

Steps to paraphrasing effectively:

1. Listen carefully to the message.
2. _____.
3. If you believe a paraphrase is necessary, restate the message to show the meaning you have received.

AN OUTLINE OF "PARAPHRASING"

Paraphrasing is a way to make a message clear by putting your understanding of it into words.

Two types of paraphrases (which can be used separately or together):

1. Content paraphrase: summarizes the meaning of the words
2. Feelings paraphrase: expresses what you understand the person's emotions to be, based on nonverbal clues

When to paraphrase

1. When you need a better understanding of a message, in terms of content and/or feelings
2. When you think you understand but you're not sure
3. When you think what was said is not what the person meant to say because of its controversial nature or the person's emotional strain
4. When your own strong reaction might have interfered with your interpretation
5. When the language being spoken is not your or the speaker's first language

How to paraphrase

1. Listen carefully to the message.
2. Determine what it means to you.
3. If you believe a paraphrase is necessary, restate the message to show the meaning you have received.

A QUIZ ON "PARAPHRASING"

Check what you've learned in taking notes on "Paraphrasing" by answering the following questions.

_____ 1. Paraphrasing means
   A. putting your understanding of someone else's message into words.
   B. putting your own message into words.
   C. listening very carefully to someone else's message.

_____ 2. A feelings paraphrase
   A. summarizes the meaning of someone's words.
   B. expresses what you understand to be the emotions behind a message.
   C. expresses your own feelings about another person's message.

_____ 3. TRUE OR FALSE? A content paraphrase and a feelings paraphrase should never be used together.

_____ 4. One good time to paraphrase is
   A. after every message that is received.
   B. after every few sentences of a message that is received.
   C. when you have a strong reaction to what the person has said.

_____ 5. The first step in paraphrasing a message is to
   A. try to guess what the message will be.
   B. listen carefully to the message.
   C. decide what the message means to you.

ANSWERS TO THE QUIZZES ON THE THREE ADDITIONAL READINGS

Quiz on "Class Profiles"

- C   lower-upper class
- E   upper-middle class
- D   lower-middle class
- A   working class
- B   lower class

Quiz on "Food Choices"

1. B
2. A
3. C
4. C
5. C

Quiz on "Paraphrasing"

1. A
2. B
3. F
4. C
5. B

TEST BANKS

This section contains the following:

- A **First Test Bank** (pages 57–144), consisting of four additional mastery tests for each chapter in Part One of *Ten Steps to Building College Reading Skills*, Fourth Edition, as well as four additional combined-skills mastery tests. These tests are similar to the end-of-chapter mastery tests in the book.
- A **Second Test Bank** (pages 151–198), consisting of two additional mastery tests for each skill and for the combined skills. These tests contain ten items each.

Instructors whose students are using *Ten Steps to Building College Reading Skills*, Fourth Edition, in class have permission to reproduce any of these tests on a photocopying machine as often as needed.

The answer key for the First Test Bank is on pages 145–149; for the Second Test Bank, on pages 199–200.

DICTIONARY USE: Test A

A. Below are five pairs of dictionary guidewords followed by a series of other words. Circle the **two** words in each series that would be found on the page with the guidewords.

1–2. **earth science / echo**

earthworm   each   easy   earthquake   eel

3–4. **glib / gloom**

gist   glide   gloat   goatee   glossy

5–6. **hiccup / high-rise**

hippie   hide-out   hockey   horseradish   hi-fi

7–8. **roar / roll**

roadrunner   rock 'n' roll   romantic   roger   rookie

9–10. **thunderhead / tide**

termite   throb   Thursday   tidy   tiddlywinks

B. Use your dictionary and the spelling hints on page 38 of the textbook to find the correct spellings of the following words.

11. occupashun _____

12. canser _____

13. errer _____

14. millitary _____

15. mistery _____

(Continues on next page)

C. Use the pronunciation key to answer the questions below.

Pronunciation Key

ă hat	ā pay	âr care	ä card	ĕ ten	ē she	ĭ sit
ī hi	îr here	ŏ lot	ō go	ô all	oi oil	ou out
ŏŏ look	yŏŏ cure	ōō cool	yōō use	ŭ up	ûr fur	th thick
th then	ə ago, item, easily, gallop, circus					

16. The *e* in *cell* (sĕl) is pronounced
    like the *e* in what common word? _____

17. The *y* in *ruby* (rōō′bē) is pronounced
    like the *e* in what common word? _____

18. The *a* in *Mars* (märz) is pronounced
    like the *a* in what common word? _____

19. The *u* in *dumpling* (dŭmp′lĭng) is pronounced
    like the *u* in what common word? _____

20. The *u* in *immunity* (ĭ-myōō′nĭ-tē) is pronounced
    like the *u* in what common word? _____

DICTIONARY USE: Test B

A. Place dots between the syllables in the following words. Then write the correct pronunciation symbols, including the accent marks. Use your dictionary.

1. m a r k e t _____

2. s t i c k u p _____

3. z i p p e r _____

4. d i m i n i s h _____

5. p e s t i c i d e _____

B. Answer the questions about the four words below. The pronunciation key on page 40 of the textbook will help you answer some of the questions.

choir (kwīr)	**log•ic** (lŏj′ĭk)
in•ven•tion (ĭn-vĕn′shən)	**moon•struck** (mōōn′strŭk′)

6. Which **two** words have the sound of *i* as in *sit*?

_____   _____

7. Which word has the sound of *o* as in *lot*? _____

8. Which word has the schwa sound? _____

9. Which word has a primary and secondary accent? _____

10. Which words have two syllables? _____

C. Use your dictionary to list the parts of speech for the following words.

11. reason _____

12. cool _____

13. one _____

14. under _____

15. advance _____

(Continues on next page)

D. Use your dictionary to write the irregular plural forms for the following words.

16. volcano _____

17. family _____

18. half _____

19. tooth _____

20. mouse _____

DICTIONARY USE: Test C

A. Answer the questions that follow the dictionary entries. The pronunciation key below will help you answer the pronunciation questions.

Pronunciation Key

ă hat	ā pay	âr **care**	ä card	ĕ ten	ē she	ĭ sit
ī hi	îr **here**	ŏ lot	ō go	ô all	oi **oil**	ou **out**
ŏŏ look	yŏŏ **cure**	ōō **cool**	yōō **use**	ŭ up	ûr **fur**	th **thick**
th **then**	ə **ago, item, easily, gallop, circus**					

ar•row (ăr′ō) *n.* **1.** A straight, thin shaft that is shot from a bow and usually made of light wood with a pointed head at one end and flight-stabilizing feathers at the other. **2.** Something similar to an arrow in form, function, or speed. **3.** A sign or symbol shaped like an arrow and used to indicate direction.

_____ 1. The *a* in *arrow* is pronounced like the *a* in
   A. *hat.*
   B. *pay.*

_____ 2. The *o* in *arrow* is pronounced like the *o* in
   A. *lot.*
   B. *go.*

_____ 3. *Arrow* is accented on
   A. the first syllable.
   B. the second syllable.

_____ 4. Which definition best fits the sentence below—definition 1, 2, or 3?

   To reach Pizza Palace, take the first right after the intersection, and then follow the *arrows* to the parking lot.

_____ 5. Which definition best fits the quotation below—definition 1, 2, or 3?

   I shot an *arrow* in the air,
   It fell to earth, I knew not where.

   —*Henry Wadsworth Longfellow*

(Continues on next page)

di•vert (dĭ-vûrt′ *or* dī-vûrt′) *v.* **-vert•ed, -vert•ing, -verts.** **1.** To turn aside from a course or direction. **2.** To distract or draw one's attention. **3.** To give pleasure by distracting the attention from worries; amuse. **—di•vert′er** *n.* **— di•vert′ing•ly** *adv.*

_____ 6. Which guidewords would be on the dictionary page with *divert*?
     A. disturb / diversity   C. divest / divulge
     B. ditzy / divide

_____ 7. How many ways can the *i* in *divert* be pronounced?
     A. One   C. Three
     B. Two

_____ 8. How many syllables does the adverb form of *divert* have?
     A. One   C. Three
     B. Two   D. Four

_____ 9. Which definition of *divert* fits the sentence below—definition 1, 2, or 3?

I went to a movie to *divert* myself from worrying about starting my new job the next day.

_____ 10. Which definition of *divert* fits the sentence below—definition 1, 2, or 3?

The policeman *diverted* the traffic onto a side street until the tow-truck had removed the broken-down bus.

B. Use your dictionary and the spelling hints on page 38 of the textbook to find the correct spellings of the following words.

11. seazon _____

12. believible _____

13. emerjancy _____

14. governer _____

15. indiferant _____

C. Place dots between the syllables in the following words. Then write the correct pronunciation symbols, including the accent marks. Use your dictionary.

16. n i f t y _____

17. f r u g a l _____

18. f o r f e i t _____

19. f e a t h e r b r a i n _____

20. s t e r e o t y p e _____

Name _____

Section _____ Date _____

SCORE: (Number correct) × 5 = _____ %

DICTIONARY USE: Test D

A. Answer the questions that follow the dictionary entries. The pronunciation key below will help you answer the pronunciation questions.

Pronunciation Key

ă hat	ā pay	âr **care**	ä **card**	ĕ ten	ē she	ĭ sit
ī hi	îr **here**	ŏ lot	ō go	ô **all**	oi **oil**	ou **out**
ŏŏ **look**	yŏŏ **cure**	ōō **cool**	yōō **use**	ŭ **up**	ûr **fur**	th **thick**
th **then**	ə **ago, item, easily, gallop, circus**					

flop (flŏp) *v.* **flopped, flop•ping, flops 1.** To fall or lie down heavily and noisily. **2.** To move about loosely or limply. **3.** *Informal.* To fail completely. **4.** *Slang.* To go to bed. —*n.* **1.** The sound made when flopping. **2.** *Informal.* A complete failure.

_____ 1. How many definitions does the verb form of *flop* have?
    A. One   C. Three
    B. Two   D. Four

_____ 2. Which guidewords would be on the dictionary page with *flop*?
    A. flop-house/Florida   C. flirt/flog
    B. flock/florid

_____ 3. In the sentence below, the definition of *flop* that applies is
    A. verb definition 1.   C. noun definition 1.
    B. verb definition 2.   D. noun definition 2.

    The TV show was a *flop*; the network cancelled it after the second week.

_____ 4. In the sentence below, the definition of *flop* that applies is
    A. verb definition 1.   D. noun definition 1.
    B. verb definition 2.   E. noun definition 2.
    C. verb definition 3.

    After the long walk in the hot sun, the exhausted dog staggered into the kitchen and *flopped* on the cool floor.

_____ 5. In the sentence below, the definition of *flop* that applies is
    A. verb definition 2.   D. noun definition 1.
    B. verb definition 3.   E. noun definition 2.
    C. verb definition 4.

    The clown's baggy pants were so long that the cuffs *flopped* around his huge shoes as he walked.

(Continues on next page)

mod•er•ate (mŏd′ər-ĭt) *adj.* **1.** Within reasonable limits; not excessive. **2.** Not subject to extremes; mild or calm. **3.** Opposed to radical or extreme views, especially in politics or religion. —*v.* (mŏd′ə-rāt′) **-at•ed, -at•ing, -ates 1.** To become less violent, severe, or extreme. **2.** To preside over or act as chairman of.

_____ 6. The *a* in the adjective *moderate* is pronounced like
A. the *i* in *sit*.   B. the *i* in *hi*.   C. the *a* in *hat*.

_____ 7. The *a* in the verb *moderate* is pronounced like the *a* in
A. the *a* in *hat*.   B. the *a* in *pay*.   C. the *a* in *card*.

_____ 8. Which syllable has the strongest accent in the verb form of *moderate*?
A. The first   B. The second   C. The third

_____ 9. In the sentence below, the definition of *moderate* that applies is
A. adjective definition 1.   D. verb definition 1.
B. adjective definition 2.   E. verb definition 2.
C. adjective definition 3.

We've had high winds and bitterly cold temperatures for the past five days, but the newspaper says we will have more *moderate* weather by the end of the week.

_____10. In the sentence below, the definition of *moderate* that applies is
A. adjective definition 1.   D. verb definition 1.
B. adjective definition 2.   E. verb definition 2.
C. adjective definition 3.

The TV anchorman was asked to *moderate* the first of the televised debates between the two presidential candidates.

B. Use your dictionary to write the irregular plural forms for the following words.

11. hero _____   13. calf _____

12. city _____   14. sister-in-law _____

C. Using your dictionary, write the pronunciation and meaning of the boldfaced word in each sentence. Make sure that you choose the definition that best fits the sentence.

15–16. "I'm rather **partial** to broccoli," Uncle Rick said, as he helped himself to his third serving.
A. Pronunciation: _____

B. Definition: _____

17–18. The company **sandbagged** the employees into working overtime by threatening to fire them.
A. Pronunciation: _____

B. Definition: _____

19–20. I had expected my grandmother's eighty-ninth birthday party to be pretty **tame**, but it turned out to be the wildest celebration I'd ever been to.
A. Pronunciation: _____

B. Definition: _____

VOCABULARY IN CONTEXT: Test A

A. For each item below, underline the **examples** that suggest the meaning of the italicized word. Then, in the space provided, write the letter of the meaning of that word.

___ 1. Joan loves to buy *exotic* foods: vegetables and herbs from China, spices from India, olives from Greece, and cheeses from France.
   A. Chinese
   B. healthy
   C. common
   D. foreign

___ 2. Unskilled workers must often take jobs that are *tedious,* such as washing dishes for hours or flipping burgers day after day.
   A. dangerous
   B. requiring great strength
   C. boring
   D. rare

___ 3. Emotionally disturbed people may be troubled by *morbid* thoughts. For instance, they may often think about suicide or murder.
   A. busy
   B. shy
   C. depressing
   D. practical

B. Each item below includes a word or words that are a **synonym** of the italicized word. Write the synonym of the italicized word in the space provided.

_____ 4. Barry was *ecstatic* when Lynda agreed to marry him. He was so overjoyed that he burst out singing on his way home.

_____ 5. *Rituals* are a common and important part of life. These ceremonies include marriages and funerals.

C. Each item below includes a word or words that are an **antonym** of the italicized word. Underline the antonym of each italicized word. Then write the letter of the meaning of the italicized word.

___ 6. A flashing yellow light means "slow down," but many drivers *accelerate* instead, trying to get through the intersection before the light turns red.
   A. reverse direction
   B. stop
   C. take a detour
   D. speed up

___ 7. "I'm willing to *affirm* that I was present when the crime was committed," the witness said. "But I strongly deny that I took part in it."
   A. guess
   B. state as true
   C. predict
   D. forget

(Continues on next page)

D. Use the **general sense of each sentence** to figure out the meaning of each italicized word. Then write the letter of the meaning of the italicized word.

_____ 8. An old saying is still true—"Be nice to people as you *ascend* the ladder of success. You may meet them again later, on your way down."
A. watch
B. go up
C. fall off
D. go down

_____ 9. The Navy *bestowed on* the admiral its highest honor.
A. gave to
B. demanded of
C. took away from
D. asked of

_____10. Gail and Jon don't always see eye to eye—for instance, they have *contrary* opinions about religion and politics. But still, they're a happy couple.
A. opposing
B. weak
C. the same
D. strong

VOCABULARY IN CONTEXT: Test B

A. For each item below, underline the **examples** that suggest the meaning of the italicized word. Then, in the space provided, write the letter of the meaning of that word.

____ 1. A *pessimist* expects bad news in every letter, an F on every test, and a "no" to every request.

    A. someone careless   C. someone who expects the worst

    B. someone hopeful   D. a dreamer

____ 2. The mental patient had two *delusions*. He believed that someone was plotting against him and that he was being controlled by something put into his brain.

    A. desires   C. illnesses

    B. false beliefs   D. habits

B. Each item below includes a word or words that are a **synonym** of the italicized word. Write the synonym of the italicized word in the space provided.

_____ 3. "Even when I make a perfectly simple statement," the politician complained, "the newspapers *distort* my meaning. They always twist my words."

_____ 4. Attempts are being made to *fortify* the Leaning Tower of Pisa in Italy. The authorities believe they must strengthen the tower to prevent it from eventually falling down.

_____ 5. Dr. Fell is a strong *advocate* of acupuncture. He is also a strong supporter of herbal remedies.

C. Each item below includes a word or words that are an **antonym** of the italicized word. Underline the antonym of each italicized word. Then write the letter of the meaning of the italicized word.

____ 6. Many people who suffer from shyness have a fear of being *conspicuous*. They dress in dull, quiet clothing in order to be almost unnoticeable.

    A. weak   C. unattractive

    B. attracting attention   D. happy

____ 7. Dawn cooked such an *elaborate* dinner for her friends that she had to work nonstop in the kitchen. If she had planned a simple menu, she could have relaxed and spent more time with her guests.

    A. delicious   C. expensive

    B. healthful   D. complicated

(Continues on next page)

8. "We have no time for on-the-job training here," the interviewer told Chung. "So we can't hire a *novice*. We need an expert with plenty of experience."
    A. someone with a college degree   C. beginner
    B. someone who isn't a citizen   D. retired person

D. Use the **general sense of each sentence** to figure out the meaning of each italicized word. Then write the letter of the meaning of the italicized word.

_____ 9. The efforts of the firemen to save the woman were *futile*—she was already dead.
    A. successful   C. useless
    B. early   D. too lengthy

_____10. The saying "Never put off till tomorrow what you can do today" warns that it is best not to *procrastinate*.
    A. delay   C. rush
    B. work too hard   D. confuse

VOCABULARY IN CONTEXT: Test C

Using context clues for help, write the letter of the best meaning for each italicized word.

____ 1. In Dickens's *A Christmas Carol,* the *miserly* Ebenezer Scrooge is visited by three spirits who change him into a generous man.
    A. stingy   C. wise
    B. kind   D. insane

____ 2. During the flood, people who had to leave their homes found *refuge* in the school gym, where they stayed for two days.
    A. answers   C. shelter
    B. flooding   D. towels

____ 3. To get their ideas across, textbook authors often use tables, charts, and graphs. These visual aids are an effective way to *convey* complicated information.
    A. create   C. ignore
    B. conceal   D. communicate

____ 4. At first, the surgery seemed to be successful. But several hours later, the patient's condition began to *deteriorate,* and it continued to worsen over the next days.
    A. improve   C. stay the same
    B. get worse   D. become clear

____ 5. If you're trying to give up smoking, here's a tip: Don't have any cigarettes readily *accessible.* Instead, put them all far out of reach.
    A. within reach   C. acceptable
    B. affordable   D. low tar

____ 6. The two towns are *comparable* in size; they both have a population of about twenty thousand. They are also very much alike in terms of average income.
    A. contrasting   C. similar
    B. in competition   D. unusual

____ 7. "I turn off the TV when there's a news story about a *gruesome* murder," Patrick said. "I don't want my kids to be frightened by all the gory details."
    A. recent   C. little-known
    B. probably untrue D. horrible

____ 8. *Optimists* are likely to work hard because they believe it is possible to reach high goals.
    A. one who expects disappointment   C. one who works hard
    B. one who is always puzzled   D. one who expects good things

(Continues on next page)

___ 9. In addition to his vacation, Victor can take off three "personal days." But this extra time off can be taken only for a *legitimate* reason—a medical emergency, a meeting with a child's teacher, and the like.
   A. health
   B. proper
   C. secret
   D. old

___10. A famous *anecdote* about Mark Twain illustrates his sense of humor: When a newspaper announced that he had died, he sent a telegram saying, "Reports of my death are greatly exaggerated."
   A. biography
   B. prediction
   C. brief story of an event
   D. amusing riddle

VOCABULARY IN CONTEXT: Test D

Using context clues for help, write the letter of the best meaning for each italicized word.

____ 1. When you are first trying to ice skate, you may seem hopelessly *inept.* But don't give up—with practice and patience, you will learn to skate.
    A. unskilled
    B. talented
    C. confident
    D. uninterested

____ 2. The interest in plays seems to be *universal.* Theater has developed in every culture in the world.
    A. unimportant
    B. intelligent
    C. quite rare
    D. found everywhere

____ 3. *Stereotypes* are not just racial or ethnic. Consider, for instance, the "dumb blond," the hot-tempered redhead, and the jolly fat person.
    A. facts
    B. languages
    C. groups
    D. oversimplified images

____ 4. It's a mistake to assume that if two events are *consecutive,* the first must have caused the second. For instance, Thursday does not cause Friday, and spring does not cause summer.
    A. happening at the same time
    B. happening unexpectedly
    C. happening one after the other
    D. happening daily

____ 5. In a research paper, you must *cite* your sources. You can present them in footnotes or endnotes, or in parentheses within the text itself.
    A. increase
    B. make known
    C. find
    D. remove

____ 6. Raul is an *indulgent* father. For instance, he lets his daughter stay up as late as she likes and never insists that she does her homework.
    A. seeking advice
    B. giving in to someone's wishes
    C. absent often
    D. strict

____ 7. People with red-green color blindness cannot *discriminate* between reds and greens. People with blue-yellow color blindness cannot distinguish between blues and yellows.
    A. prefer
    B. care
    C. paint
    D. tell the difference

____ 8. Both children and adults sometimes purposely act less *competent* than they really are. By pretending to be helpless, they can get others to do things for them.
    A. trusting
    B. capable
    C. nervous
    D. friendly

(Continues on next page)

_____ 9. "Necessity is the mother of invention" is an old saying. It means that when a need exists, creative minds will *devise* something to meet that need.

A. buy

C. hide

B. invent

D. oppose

_____10. Languages *evolve* over time, as you can see if you open a page of *The Canterbury Tales*, written about six hundred years ago by the English poet Chaucer. It is barely recognizable as English today.

A. remain the same

C. develop and change

B. improve

D. get worse

MAIN IDEAS: Test A

A. Each cluster of words below is made up of a general idea and four specific ideas. The general idea includes all of the specific ideas. Underline the general idea in each group.

1. sandals   footwear   sneakers   boots   high heels

2. chocolate   raspberry   lemon   butterscotch   flavor

3. button   zipper   Velcro   fastener   snap

4. actor   entertainer   dancer   singer   comedian

5. mother   father   son   granddaughter   family

6. love   hate   anger   emotion   joy

7. road   boulevard   freeway   turnpike   expressway

B. In each item below, one idea is general and the others are specific. The general idea includes the specific ones. In the spaces provided, write in two more specific ideas that are covered by the general idea.

8. *General:* apartment problems
   Specific: no hot water, broken lock,   _____, _____

9. *General:* means of transportation
   Specific: boat, airplane,   _____, _____

10. *General:* fruit
    Specific: orange, banana,   _____, _____

11. *General:* dog
    Specific: pit bull, collie,   _____, _____

12. *General:* time to give a gift
    Specific: Valentine's Day, anniversary, _____, _____

13. *General:* language
    Specific: English, Latin,   _____, _____

14. *General:* question word
    Specific: who, where,   _____, _____

15. *General:* long-term goal
    Specific: get a degree, learn French,   _____, _____

(Continues on next page)

C. In each pair below, one idea is general and the other is specific. The general idea includes the specific one. Do two things:

   a Underline the idea in each pair that you think is more general.
   b Then write in one more specific idea that is covered by the general idea.

16. punishment   hanging   _____

17. honey   sweetener   _____

18. river   body of water   _____

19. exercise   sit-up   _____

20. chore   washing dishes   _____

21. cough syrup   medicine   _____

22. difficult weather   tornado   _____

23. oak   wood   _____

24. seasoning   pepper   _____

25. symptom   cough   _____

MAIN IDEAS: Test B

A. Each cluster of words below is made up of a general idea and four specific ideas. The general idea includes all of the specific ideas. Underline the general idea in each group.

1. chapter   book   index   cover   table of contents

2. rose   daisy   tulip   flower   carnation

3. comforters   sheets   bedding   blankets   pillowcases

4. expense   food   taxes   gas   rent

5. turtle   reptile   crocodile   snake   alligator

6. elbow   wrist   joint   knee   ankle

7. oxygen   hydrogen   neon   gas   carbon monoxide

8. novelist   poet   playwright   writer   journalist

B. (9–20.) In each group below, one statement is the general point, and the other statements are specific support for the point. Identify the point with a **P** and each statement of support with an **S**.

Group 1

_____ My parents complain when I come home late.

_____ I think it's time for me to look for my own apartment.

_____ My mother wants detailed information about all the people in my life.

_____ My parents want me to start paying rent for living at home.

Group 2

_____ We can go weeks without food, but only two or three days without water.

_____ Water is needed for the body to wash away its waste products.

_____ Water is essential to the human body.

_____ Water also moistens the body's tissues so they can carry oxygen.

(Continues on next page)

Group 3

_____ The economy is in a slump.

_____ At present, unemployment is especially high.

_____ Interest rates are rising, which slows down economic growth.

_____ Many businesses have filed for bankruptcy.

MAIN IDEAS: Test C

A. In each pair below, one idea is general and the other is specific. The general idea includes the specific one. Do two things:

   a Underline the idea in each pair that you think is more general.

   b Then write in one more specific idea that is covered by the general idea.

   1. flounder   fish   _____

   2. amount   pound   _____

   3. outerwear   wool scarf   _____

   4. yogurt   dairy product   _____

   5. sofa   furniture   _____

   6. fictional character   Cinderella   _____

B. (7–10.) In the following group, one statement is the general point, and the other statements are specific support for the point. Identify the point with a P and each statement of support with an S.

   _____ The biggest female stars make less than the most famous male stars.

   _____ Very few good roles are written for older women.

   _____ The film industry tends to treat women as second-class citizens.

   _____ Only a handful of women have been allowed to direct major motion pictures.

C. (11–18.) Each group of items below includes one topic, one main idea (topic sentence), and two supporting details. In the space provided, label each item with one of the following:

T—for the topic
MI—for the main idea
SD—for the supporting details

Group 1

   _____ Young Amish boys learn to help their fathers tend crops and livestock.

   _____ Amish children are taught to assist their parents with family work.

   _____ The children in Amish families.

   _____ Amish girls are taught to help their mothers cook, clean, and sew.

(Continues on next page)

Group 2

_____ Lloyd's of London's insurance policies.

_____ Fred Astaire had his legs insured for $650,000.

_____ One model was insured against "worry lines" on the face.

_____ Lloyd's of London has sold some odd insurance policies.

D. Read the passage below and then answer the questions that follow.

[1]To describe the business of marketing, we can use the A-T-R theory. [2]According to that theory, there are three stages in selling a product: Awareness, Trial, and Reinforcement. [3]The first stage, awareness of a product, is achieved through advertising. [4]To bring about the second stage, the trial, many companies give away free samples or coupons. [5]Finally, reinforcement involves constantly reminding the consumer to try the product again.

_____ 19. The list words that signal the main idea of the paragraph are
  A. *the A-T-R theory.*
  B. *three stages.*
  C. *free samples or coupons.*

_____ 20. The addition words that introduce the major details of the paragraph are
  A. *business, theory, selling.*
  B. *according, the, to bring about.*
  C. *first, second, finally.*

MAIN IDEAS: Test D

A. (1–4.) The following group of items includes one topic, one main idea (topic sentence), and two supporting details. In the space provided, label each item with one of the following:

T—for the topic
MI—for the main idea
SD—for the supporting details

_____ The ancient Aztecs of Mexico.

_____ The Aztecs practiced bloody human sacrifice, but they also valued such gentle arts as poetry.

_____ The Aztecs were fierce soldiers, but they were also skilled farmers who knew how to bring water to the desert and how to grow crops on wetlands.

_____ The Aztec culture included surprising contradictions.

B. Write the letter of the correct topic of each of the following paragraphs. Then find the sentence in which the author states the main idea about that topic, and write that number in the space provided.

Paragraph 1

¹John Fitzgerald Kennedy was made for television. ²His tall, thin body gave him the strong vertical line that cameras love, and his weatherbeaten good looks appealed to women and men. ³He had a full head of hair, and even in the winter he maintained a tan. ⁴In addition, he was always "cool" in public. ⁵This too was tailor-made for the "cool medium," television. ⁶Wit, irony, and understatement, all delivered casually, translate well on television.

____ 5. The topic is
    A. politicians.
    B. John F. Kennedy.
    C. President Kennedy's wit.

____ 6. Write the number of the sentence that states the main idea of the paragraph.

(Continues on next page)

Paragraph 2

¹In 1801, a candidate for Congress challenged to a duel an Army officer who called him "a bowl of skimmed milk." ²At that duel, the two men killed each other. ³Newspaper editors were challenged so often that many put on their pistols when they dressed in the morning. ⁴In Vicksburg, Mississippi, three newspaper editors died in duels in the 1840s. ⁵These examples indicate that as recently as the 1800s, dueling with weapons was a common way to defend one's honor.

_____ 7. The topic is
  A. ways to defend one's honor.
  B. newspaper editors' dueling to defend their honor.
  C. dueling to defend one's honor.

_____ 8. Write the number of the sentence that states the main idea of the paragraph.

Paragraph 3

¹Shakespeare wrote that "all the world's a stage." ²He meant that everyone has at least one part, or role, to play in life. ³In fact, every role we play has an "on stage" and a "backstage" area; in the first area, we're on our best behavior; but in the second area, we can "let our hair down." ⁴For example, in the dining room, a waiter is "on stage." ⁵No matter how rushed he is or how annoyed he feels, a waiter is expected to be polite and helpful to his customers. ⁶Once he returns to the kitchen, however, it's another matter. ⁷There he is "backstage" and can let his true feelings show. ⁶In the kitchen, the waiter can make sarcastic remarks about the customers or even joke about serving a plate of food that's been dropped.

_____ 9. The topic is
  A. "on stage" and "backstage" roles.
  B. human behavior.
  C. "backstage" behavior.

_____10. Write the number of the sentence that states the main idea of the paragraph.

SUPPORTING DETAILS: Test A

A. (1–5.) Complete the outline below by filling in the missing major details. Then answer the question that follows the outline.

[1]Research suggests ways in which parents can encourage creativity in children. [2]One way is to provide a stimulating environment. [3]As much as possible, the environment should be designed to match a child's special interests and talents. [4]Second, teach by focusing on a child's strengths. [5]Avoid criticizing his or her weaknesses. [6]Another important method is to encourage nonconforming behavior. [7]You can do this by helping your children avoid or resist peer pressure. [8]Fourth, set an example by pursuing interesting work or intellectual or artistic hobbies. [9]Finally, do not use rigid control over children. [10]Children who are constantly directed seem to lose the confidence needed for the creative spirit.

Main idea: Research suggests ways in which parents can encourage creativity in children.

1. _____

2. _____

3. Encourage nonconforming behavior.

4. _____

5. _____

5. What words in the main idea tell us that a list is coming?

_____

(Continues on next page)

B. (6–10.) Complete the map by finishing the heading and filling in the missing major details. Then answer the questions that follow the map.

[1]Several different factors influence people's eating habits. [2]Personal preference is one of the most important factors that determines what people eat. [3]Almost all people enjoy the sweetness of sugar and the tang of salt. [4]Others like spices such as the hot peppers common in Mexican food or curry popular in Indian dishes. [5]Another factor that influences eating is culture. [6]People often like to eat the foods they grew up eating. [7]And every country—and region of a country—has its own special foods and ways of combining foods into meals. [8]Economics is a third issue that affects what and how people eat. [9]Foods that are readily available at low cost often become part of people's diets. [10]Likewise, meals made with expensive or hard-to-get ingredients are rarely eaten, if at all.

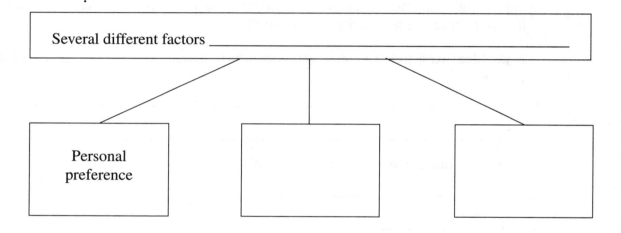

9. What addition word introduces the second major detail? _____

10. What addition word signals the third major detail? _____

SUPPORTING DETAILS: Test B

A. (1–4.) Complete the outline below by filling in the major details. Include brief explanations for each, as shown for the first major detail.

> [1]Three broad types of leadership have been identified. [2]First is the autocratic style. [3]The autocratic leader centralizes authority and does not involve others in decision making. [4]This manager uses authority in a straightforward manner. [5]He or she simply issues orders. [6]A second type of leader is the democratic leader. [7]The democratic leader shares authority and involves employees in decision making. [8]He or she encourages employee participation and communication. [9]At the same time, this type of leader makes it clear that he or she has the final say. [10]Finally, the "hands off" leader leads by taking the role of consultant. [11]He or she provides encouragement for employees' ideas and offers insights or opinions when asked.

Main idea: Three broad types of leadership have been identified.

1. _____—simply issues orders.

2. _____

   _____

3. _____

   _____

4. What word or words in the main idea tell us that a list is coming?

   _____

(Continues on next page)

B. (5–10.) Fill in the major details and examples needed to complete the map below. Then answer the questions that follow the map.

^{1}People who have common concerns or points of view are called interests, and the groups that organize them are called interest groups. ^{2}There are two general types of interest groups. ^{3}One is special interest groups. ^{4}They are groups that mainly seek benefits from which their members would gain more than the society as a whole. ^{5}Examples include chambers of commerce, trade associations, labor unions, and farm organizations. ^{6}The second type of interest group is public interest groups. ^{7}These are groups which pursue policies that are thought to be of no greater benefit to their members than to the larger society. ^{8}Consumer protection organizations are good examples of public interest groups.

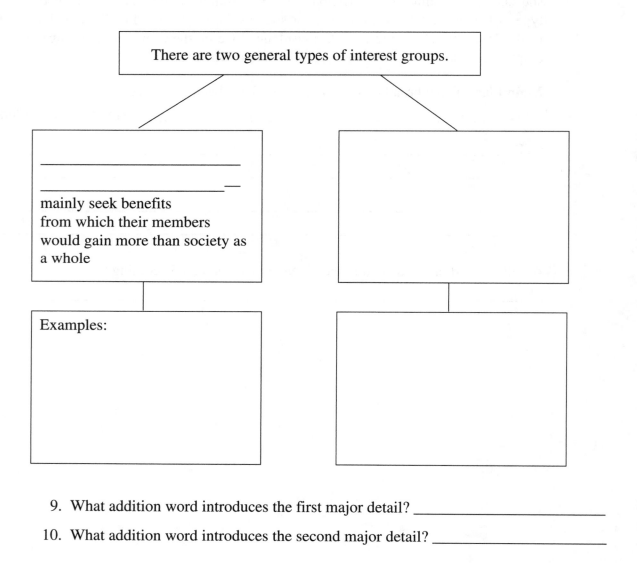

9. What addition word introduces the first major detail? _____

10. What addition word introduces the second major detail? _____

SUPPORTING DETAILS: Test C

A. (1–6.) Complete the outline below by filling in the missing major and minor details. Some details have been filled in for you. (You may find it helpful to mark off with a check or number the major details in the paragraph.)

¹Having to give a speech or report in front of a group of other people can be a frightening experience, but there are ways you can make it more bearable. ²One way to reduce your fear is to choose a topic you know something about and are interested in. ³If you are comfortable with your topic, you will feel more relaxed when you are in front of an audience. ⁴You will also have more confidence in your ability to say something worthwhile on a topic you care about. ⁵A second key in controlling nervousness is to prepare well for your speech. ⁶Take time to organize your points so your audience can learn what you want them to know. ⁷Also, rehearse your speech several times so you will feel confident you know it well. ⁸A third way to deal with your fear is to practice relaxation activities just before it is time to deliver your speech. ⁹On the day of your speech, try to clear your mind, telling yourself you have done all you can to prepare yourself. ¹⁰Then, as you approach the speaker's stand, take a deep breath and smile, reminding yourself that in a few minutes your speech will be over.

Main idea: There are ways to make giving a speech more bearable.

1. Choose a topic _____.

    a. Feeling more comfortable with your topic will make you feel more relaxed in front of an audience.

    b. You will also have more confidence in your ability to say something worthwhile on a topic you care about.

2. _____

    a. _____

    b. _____

3. _____

    a. _____

    b. As you approach the speaker's stand, take a deep breath, smile, and remind yourself that in a few minutes, your speech will be over.

(Continues on next page)

B. (7–10.) Complete the main idea and fill in the major details needed to complete the map below.

[1]The level of stress in working parents can be high. [2]Professionals, however, offer several suggestions on how to help keep the demands of home and job in balance. [3]First of all, set limits. [4]This means to set aside time to relax and enjoy yourself. [5]Another helpful suggestion is to make frequent lists of things to do in the order of importance you give them. [6]At the top of the list may be "spend time with my children" and "go to work"; at the bottom may be "return Dora's call." [7]A third suggestion to fight stress is to ask for help. [8]Tell your spouse, partner, or children exactly what you want from them. [9]Discuss ways to share responsibilities at home. [10]It is also helpful to team up with other parents to share chores such as child care and driving kids to school. [11]Finally, say the experts, don't aim for perfection—perfection is an obstacle to reducing stress. [12]For instance, be willing to tolerate less-than-perfect results on household chores.

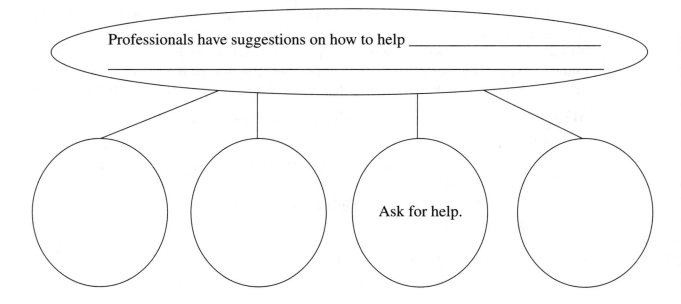

Professionals have suggestions on how to help _____ _____

Ask for help.

SUPPORTING DETAILS: Test D

A. (1–6.) Complete the outline below by filling in the missing major and minor details. Some details have been filled in for you. (You may find it helpful to mark off with a check or number the major details in the paragraph.)

¹Once a virus, bacteria, or other pathogen enters your body, you can go through the five stages of a disease. ²First is the incubation period, which begins once the disease-causing agent enters your body. ³During this time, the pathogens multiply and spread throughout your body. ⁴Next is the early-symptom stage. ⁵During this stage, the disease is highly contagious. ⁶Symptoms are usually general and mild. ⁷They can include fever, headache, sneezing and tiredness. ⁸The third stage, clinical disease, is the peak of the disease. ⁹Specific symptoms of the disease usually appear. ¹⁰For example, jaundice is a symptom of hepatitis. ¹¹Swelling of the face along the jawbone is a symptom of mumps. ¹²Because symptoms develop that a doctor can observe, the disease can usually be diagnosed during this stage. ¹³Symptoms begin to disappear in the decline stage. ¹⁴Although you start to feel better, your body is still weakened from the disease. ¹⁵You can become worse if you become too active too soon. ¹⁶Sometimes you can still transmit the disease to others during this stage. ¹⁷Convalescence is the final stage during which your body recovers. ¹⁸Most diseases are not contagious during convalescence.

Main idea: Once a virus, bacteria, or other pathogen enters your body, you can go through the five stages of a disease.

   1. Incubation period

      a. It begins once the disease-causing agent enters your body.

      b. Pathogens _____

   2. Early-symptom stage

      a. _____

      b. Symptoms are usually general and mild.

   3. Clinical disease

      a. This is the peak of the disease.

      b. Specific symptoms of the disease usually appear, allowing doctor to diagnose the illness.

   4. _____

      a. You start to feel better, but are still weak and can become worse if you become too active.

      b. _____

   5. _____

      a. Your body recovers during this stage.

      b. _____

(Continues on next page)

B. (7–10.) Fill in the major details and the one missing explanation needed to complete the map below.

¹There are three common ways people respond to those who offend or bother them. ²Perhaps the most common way people deal with such negative situations is through passive behavior. ³Passive people do not share their feelings when they are upset. ⁴Instead of trying to stop what is bothering them, passive people will often remain silent and allow others to continue their annoying behavior. ⁵A second way people deal with a negative situation is through aggressive behavior. ⁶Aggressive people lash out at those who have hurt them—with little regard for others' feelings. ⁷The third way of dealing with negative situations is through assertive behavior. ⁸Like those who are aggressive, assertive people also actively address the cause of their problem—they just do it differently. ⁹They don't yell at the person who has bothered them. ¹⁰Instead, assertive people will discuss what has annoyed them and then work to find a way to fix it.

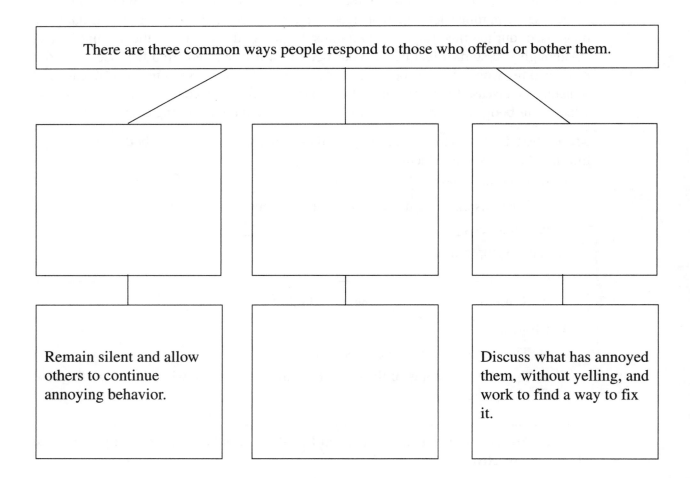

There are three common ways people respond to those who offend or bother them.

Remain silent and allow others to continue annoying behavior.

Discuss what has annoyed them, without yelling, and work to find a way to fix it.

LOCATIONS OF MAIN IDEAS: Test A

The main idea may appear at any place within each of the five paragraphs that follow. Write the number of each main idea in the space provided.

____ 1. [1]A character in a novel or a short story may be older or younger than you. [2]The character may live on a farm, while you live in a city. [3]The character may be living long ago—during the American Revolution, or in ancient Rome, or in the Middle Ages. [4]The character may be male while you are female, white while you are black, rich while you are poor—or vice versa. [5]Rarely do you meet a fictional character who is just like yourself, so when you read fiction, you must step outside the narrow boundaries of your own life.

____ 2. [1]Behavior experts think there are two main reasons why some people experience stress when buying clothes for themselves. [2]First, anxious shoppers often don't like the look of their bodies, and trying on clothes (especially in front of mirrors) makes them confront what they'd rather not think about. [3]Second, these people are sometimes unsure about what image they want to project (studious? sexy? respectable?), so it's hard for them to make clothing choices without feeling frustrated.

____ 3. [1]Blocking out your feelings may seem like a good way to protect yourself at emotionally difficult times. [2]But psychologists report that people who keep feelings locked inside are likely to run into trouble. [3]First, unexpressed emotions only deepen and become even more troubling. [4]Also, people with buried emotions often have a difficult time relating to others and are afraid of being hurt if they open up. [5]In addition, those hidden feelings may eventually find a harmful way to get out. [6]For example, people whose feelings are blocked off are more likely to have alcohol problems, attempt suicide, or try to hurt others.

____ 4. [1]Few things are more boring than standing in line. [2]Luckily, some ways have been found to make waiting in line more bearable. [3]Airlines have begun to hire experts to make sure people are waiting in the right lines, and one New York bank pays five dollars to any customer who has waited more than seven minutes. [4]Fast-food restaurants have found that timing the work of fast-food workers motivates crews to work more quickly, resulting in lines that move faster. [5]Dividing tasks so that one person takes an order while another begins to prepare it also gets food to customers more quickly. [6]In amusement parks, customers complain less when signs explain how long people can expect to wait. [7]Also, live entertainment such as a magician or juggler cheers people waiting in long lines.

(Continues on next page)

___ 5. [1]Wording with more than one meaning can unnecessarily confuse and disappoint. [2]For instance, unclear language on a menu resulted in a disappointed diner. [3]The menu listed "tostada with beans." [4]The customer, expecting a tostada with beans on the side, was disappointed to be served a tostada with beans inside of it. [5]A more serious misunderstanding occurred when a nurse told one of her patients that he "wouldn't be needing" his robe, books, and shaving materials anymore. [6]The patient became quiet and moody. [7]When the nurse asked about the odd behavior, she discovered that the poor man had interpreted her statement to mean he was going to die soon. [8]In fact, the nurse meant he would be going home shortly.

LOCATIONS OF MAIN IDEAS: Test B

The main idea may appear at any place within each of the five paragraphs that follow. Write the number of each main idea in the space provided.

____ 1. [1]By having a device called a teletypewriter, or TTY, deaf people can communicate on the telephone using the written word rather than the voice. [2]Two people with this equipment converse by dialing the phone number in the usual way. [3]Then they type out their message on the keyboard of the TTY. [4]The message is transmitted over the telephone line and gets printed out on a screen or paper, depending on the type of TTY used. [5]The receiver can then type back a message to the original caller, and so on.

____ 2. [1]Why do people go to the theater? [2]Of course, there are all sorts of individual answers to this question. [3]In general, though, theatergoers seem to have three main motives: to be entertained, to join in a shared experience, and to stretch their minds. [4]Entertainment is probably the most typical reason: most people go to a play to relax and enjoy themselves. [5]Sharing an experience is also significant. [6]At a live performance, people come together and form a group, almost a little community. [7]The third reason is important to many audience members: for them, theater is a way of enriching the mind and learning something, a source of personal growth.

____ 3. [1]In the seventeenth century, the Dutch became very fond of collecting tulip bulbs. [2]The finest bulbs gained high prices, and traders began making a profit in buying and selling them. [3]Eventually, people paid great fortunes for single tulip bulbs, kept them for a few weeks, and then sold them for even a higher price. [4]But finally, buyers realized that the bulbs were not worth the high prices demanded. [5]The great Tulip Mania came to a sudden end when prices fell greatly overnight. [6]Interest in the common Dutch tulip thus led to one of the first "crashes" in economic history.

____ 4. [1]You can help save the Earth by forming some environmentally sound habits. [2]Store foods in covered bowls instead of wrapping them in foil. [3]Write on both sides of a piece of paper, and use scrap paper for messages. [4]Turn off the water while washing dishes, brushing your teeth, or shaving. [5]Eliminate a couple of car trips per week. [6]Choose cloth diapers instead of disposable ones. [7]Avoid lawn-care chemicals, which can find their way into water supplies. [8]Also, put aluminum cans, plastic containers, and papers in recycling containers when you are finished with them.

(Continues on next page)

_____ 5. [1]People who are convicted of robbing or burglarizing strangers are likely to be sent to prison. [2]But policemen and prosecutors tend to regard crimes between acquaintances less seriously than other crimes. [3]For example, suppose that Joe and Dan know each other. [4]Dan steals Joe's TV set, and claims he did it because Joe didn't pay back money that Dan had lent him. [5]This is likely to be regarded as a sort of private matter—Joe may not be considered altogether innocent by the police and prosecutor. [6]And Dan is less likely to be sent to prison than if he had stolen the TV from someone he didn't know.

LOCATIONS OF MAIN IDEAS: Test C

The main idea may appear at any place within each of the five paragraphs that follow. Write the number of each main idea in the space provided.

____ 1. [1]If a naked woman rode down your street on a horse, could you resist taking a look? [2]That's the decision a tailor in Coventry, England, had to make in the eleventh century. [3]The governor of his town was making the people pay too much in taxes. [4]The governor's wife, Godiva, asked him to have mercy on the people. [5]He agreed to be more merciful if she would ride through the streets naked, and that's what Lady Godiva did. [6]All the people in town covered their windows so that they would not embarrass the lady. [7]But one tailor, Tom, took a look. [8]And so ever since Lady Godiva's naked ride, the term "peeping Tom" has meant someone who watches people secretly.

____ 2. [1]Children who are neglected or abused in early childhood can be damaged to a degree that can never be fully repaired. [2]One little girl known as Anna is a sad example. [3]Anna was the child of a young unmarried woman living in a rural area in the 1940s. [4]The child's mother confined her to a dark attic room, where she was given enough milk to live, but almost no human contact. [5]When Anna was 6, she was discovered by the authorities and placed in a foster home. [6]At that time, she appeared to be deaf and profoundly mentally retarded, being unable to walk, talk, or even chew. [7]Eventually Anna began to learn to walk and talk, but she never achieved anything approaching normal development. [8]Her early malnutrition led to her death at age 11.

____ 3. [1]A conflict can exist only when both parties are aware of a disagreement. [2]For instance, you may be upset for months because a neighbor's loud stereo keeps you awake at night, but no conflict exists between the two of you until the neighbor learns of your problem. [3]Of course, you can communicate your displeasure with somebody without saying a word. [4]A dirty look, the silent treatment, or avoiding the other person are all ways of expressing yourself.

____ 4. [1]Before the 1840s, schools were quite limited in terms of the numbers who attended and the quality of education. [2]Apprenticeship was a major form of education. [3]Formal schooling was largely available to those who could afford to pay. [4]Even "free" schools often required the payment of tuition. [5]And primary schools often required entering students to already be able to read. [6]This policy kept out students who had not been taught to read by their parents. [7]Many schools admitted pupils regardless of age, mixing young children with young adults. [8]Classrooms could contain as many as eighty pupils. [9]Few textbooks were available, and most learning amounted to monotonous repetition of facts. [10]School buildings were generally unpainted, overcrowded, and lacked chalkboards or windows.

(Continues on next page)

___ 5. [1]Over the ages, many cultures have considered it better to be right-handed than left-handed. [2]And it is true that being left-handed has disadvantages, such as being more prone to allergies. [3]However, left-handedness does have advantages. [4]Benjamin Franklin, Leonardo da Vinci, and Pablo Picasso were all left-handed. [5]All these men (males are more likely than females to favor the left hand) had a highly developed ability to visualize space. [6]That ability is a quality that may be stronger in left-handed people. [7]This fact may explain the high proportion of left-handed architects. [8]Also, left-handed people may actually be more likely to have special intellectual gifts. [9]A study of over 100,000 twelve- and thirteen-year-olds found nearly 300 who scored very high on the Scholastic Aptitude Test (SAT). [10]Twenty percent of this top-scoring group were left-handed, twice the rate of left-handedness in the general population.

Name _____

Section _____ Date _____

SCORE: (Number correct) × 20 = _____ %

LOCATIONS OF MAIN IDEAS: Test D

The main idea may appear at any place within each of the five paragraphs that follow. Write the number of each main idea in the space provided.

____ 1. [1]In African cultures, music is a very important part of life, with many functions. [2]Music is used for entertainment, for dancing, in plays, and in ceremonies. [3]It also marks specific life events such as birth, coming of age, marriage, and death. [4]Music often accompanies work, with special songs for, say, chopping wood, rowing a boat, and harvesting crops. [5]There are even special songs for when people are suing each other in a law court. [6]And music is also a way of communicating—songs are used to pass on a group's history and to report and comment on current news.

____ 2. [1]In naturally stressful situations, the time of greatest stress is not necessarily the time when danger is at its height. [2]This fact is illustrated by a research study of the pattern of stress on a group of twenty-eight parachutists. [3]Each man was asked to describe his feelings before, during, and after his jump. [4]All reported an increase of fear and of desire to escape as the time for the jump approached. [5]Once the men were in line and realized that they could not turn back, however, they began to calm down. [6]By the time they reached the most dangerous part of the jump—when they were in free fall and waiting for their chutes to open—they had calmed down.

____ 3. [1]When you're embarrassed or ashamed, your face turns red. [2]When you're frightened, you grow pale. [3]Both blushing and turning pale are the result of activity in your nervous system. [4]Certain nerves react to your emotional state. [5]Those nerves in turn affect the tiny blood vessels in your face and neck. [6]When those vessels grow larger, allowing more blood to flow through them, you blush. [7]When they become smaller, the blood supply is lessened. [8]Then you grow pale.

____ 4. [1]Have you ever wondered why some animals, including human beings, walk upright instead of on all fours? [2]For one thing, bipedalism—walking on two feet rather than four—makes an animal taller and thus able to see farther. [3]This helps the animal to spot danger and food or water sooner. [4]Also, a taller animal can stretch higher for foods, such as eggs in birds' nests or nuts and fruits growing on trees. [5]Second, bipedalism frees the front limbs for use as arms and hands rather than as legs and and feet; this means that the animal can grasp and carry objects and, most important, use tools. [6]Thus walking on two feet has important advantages for well-being and even survival.

(Continues on next page)

___ 5. [1]A sole proprietorship is a business owned by one person. [2]It is one of the most common forms of business ownership. [3]Sole proprietorship has both advantages and disadvantages. [4]One advantage is ease of starting. [5]All you have to do to begin a sole proprietorship is to obtain any necessary licenses, open your doors, and start selling your goods or services. [6]Once you're under way, you have the satisfaction of working for yourself. [7]You can make your own decisions—what hours to work, whom to hire, what prices to charge, and so on. [8]Best of all, you can keep all the profits, assuming there are any. [9]However, sole proprietorships are usually quite small since a single person's financial resources are likely to be limited. [10]Furthermore, sole proprietors are financially fully responsible for their businesses. [11]They may even have to sell their family home to satisfy a business debt.

RELATIONSHIPS I: Test A

A. Fill in each blank with the appropriate transition word or words from the box. Use each transition once. Then, in the space provided, write the letter of the transition you have chosen.

A. after	B. another	C. first
D. in addition	E. later	

___ 1. ¹Francis Scott Key wrote "The Star-Spangled Banner" in 1814. ²(He took the melody from an eighteenth-century drinking song). ³Over a century _____, in 1931, the song was adopted as the national anthem by the United States Congress.

___ 2. ¹Before reading your first assignment in a textbook, acquaint yourself with the format and content of the book. ²_____, read the table of contents. ³Next, skim the book, looking for ways the author organizes information and highlights important points.

___ 3. ¹Birds make certain sounds to communicate with their young. ²They also make calls that signal the presence of food. ³_____, birds cry out alarms to warn their flock to take to the air.

___ 4. ¹Leaders have several qualities. ²Surveys have found that most formal leaders are above average in height. ³_____ common quality of leaders is enthusiasm.

___ 5. ¹A well-known psychologist suggested that humans seek to satisfy a series of needs, including those for food, sleep, and spirituality. ²Higher-level needs can be fulfilled only _____ the more basic ones have been met.

(Continues on next page)

B. Fill in each blank with one of the transitions in the box. Use each transition once. Then answer the question that follows.

after	another	finally
one		

¹Have you ever had trouble remembering information despite hours of studying? ²This trouble may make your studying a frustrating experience. ³However, there are a number of methods you can use to improve your memory—and your test scores. ⁴(6)_____ method is to overlearn information. ⁵This means that ⁶(7)_____ you feel that you really know the material, you should still review it one to three more times. ⁷(8)_____ good method is to organize and categorize information. ⁸Many students take notes on class material but fail to organize it into more easily learned lists or steps. ⁹(9)_____, you should interact in some way with the information you have learned. ¹⁰For example, if you take notes on and outline a biology chapter, you will understand and remember it better than if you had just tried to memorize parts of it.

____10. The main pattern of organization of the above paragraph is
  A. list of items.
  B. time order.

RELATIONSHIPS I: Test B

A. Write the letter of the answer that describes the relationship indicated by the italicized transition.

____ 1. *During* a tornado, winds can reach over one hundred miles an hour.

The relationship of the two parts of the sentence is one of
A. addition.   B. time.

____ 2. [1]In April 1961, the Russians launched the first manned satellite. [2]Less than a month *later,* on May 5, 1961, American Alan B. Shepard was sent into space for a fifteen-minute flight.

The relationship of the second sentence to the first is one of
A. addition.   B. time.

____ 3. [1]There are several ways to save money on your weekly grocery bill. [2]First, look for sales. [3]Next, clip and use coupons. [4]*Third,* buy as many items as you can in large economy sizes.

The relationship of the last sentence to the previous sentences is one of
A. addition.   B. time.

____ 4. *After* the Civil War, there were no laws to protect the consumer from false claims for ineffective or even dangerous medicines.

The relationship of the two parts of the sentence is one of
A. addition.   B. time.

____ 5. [1]To make your writing more clear, use words that your readers are likely to understand. [2]*Also,* use transitions to help your reader understand the relationships between ideas.

The relationship of the second sentence to the first sentence is one of
A. addition.   B. time.

B. Read the passage and then answer the question that follows.

[1]Most people would agree that the more variety there is in a fireworks display, the better. [2]There are actually four different types of fireworks available. [3]The first type, skyrockets, explode high in the air and produce the most dramatic effects. [4]These are the fireworks that are most likely to produce "oohs" and "aahs" from the crowd. [5]The next type, Roman candles, shoot out separate groups of sparks and colored flames. [6]This display is accompanied by a series of loud booming noises. [7]The third type, pinwheels, throw off sparks and flames as they whirl on the end of a stick. [8]Finally, lances are thin, colorful fireworks used in ground displays.

____ 6. The main pattern of organization of the above paragraph is
A. list of items.
B. time order.

(Continues on next page)

C. Fill in each blank with the appropriate transition word from the box. Use each transition once. Then answer the question that follows.

during	final	next

[1]A supervisor must sometimes counsel employees about certain long-term practices that must change for the good of the company. [2]Such problems include drug abuse, frequent errors, and tardiness. [3]There are four stages in the process of counseling employees. [4]The first stage is identifying the problem. [5](7)_____ this stage, the supervisor helps the employee identify and explain a problem and its causes. [6]The second stage is seeing how determined the employee is. [7]If he or she shows little or no interest in solving the problem, it's time to consider removing that person from the organization. [8]If, however, the employee shows some desire to solve the problem, then the supervisor should move on to the (8)_____ stage. [9]Stage three is solving the problem. [10]The problem will be solved more effectively if the employee is involved in creating and evaluating methods of correction. [11]The (9)_____ stage is following up on the solution. [12]The supervisor and employee meet again at a specified time to review the results of their action plan. [13]If the situation has improved, then praise or some other reward is in order. [14]If it has not changed or has worsened, then the next meeting must once again emphasize the problem and its consequences.

____10. The main pattern of organization of the above paragraph is
    A. list of items.
    B. time order.

RELATIONSHIPS I: Test C

Read each textbook passage and answer the questions or follow the directions provided.

A. [1]A psychologist has identified three elements in attitudes. [2]The first element is beliefs. [3]They are your basic values. [4]For example, if good health is one of your values, you probably believe people should exercise. [5]The second element of attitudes is emotions. [6]Emotions are what separate attitudes from opinions. [7]Suppose someone asked a woman if she thought colleges should have books on earthquakes. [8]She replies, "Sure," and then goes on with her daily activities. [9]Her opinion is pro-education, but she does not have any emotions about knowledge of earthquakes. [10]However, if she became upset about the lack of library books on earthquakes, her opinion would be developing into an attitude. [11]Because attitudes and emotions go together, there is almost always some form of behavioral result, so the third element of attitudes is behavior. [12]For example, if you feel strongly about an issue, you might write a letter or contribute to a campaign.

____ 1. The main pattern of organization of the above selection is
   A. list of items.
   B. time order.

2–3. Two of the transitions that signal major details of the paragraph are

_____ and _____ .

B. [1]Cardiopulmonary resuscitation (CPR) is a simple technique involving just a few steps. [2]First, open the victim's mouth and be certain that the mouth, nose and throat are free of any obstructions. [3]Then begin artificial breathing by blowing into the victim's mouth while keeping the nostrils closed with your fingers. [4]Next, check to see if there is a pulse. [5]Finally, if there is no pulse, begin a rhythmic pumping action on the chest over the heart to restore circulation.

____ 4. The main pattern of organization of the above selection is
   A. list of items.
   B. time order.

5. The words that introduce the major supporting details of the passage are *first, then,*

_____ , and *finally.*

(Continues on next page)

C. [1]We generally think of listening as a single activity. [2]However, there are four different types of listening. [3]The first type is appreciative listening. [4]It is done for pleasure or enjoyment, such as when we listen to music or a comedy routine. [5]The second type is empathic listening, which provides emotional support for the speaker, such as when we lend an ear to a friend in need. [6]The third type, comprehensive listening, is used to understand the message of a speaker. [7]This type of listening occurs, for example, when we attend a classroom lecture or listen to directions to find a friend's house. [8]The final type of listening is critical listening, which we use to evaluate a message for acceptance or rejection. [9]We use critical listening when we judge the sales pitch of a used-car dealer or the campaign speech of a political candidate.

____ 6. The main pattern of organization of the above paragraph is
   A. list of items.
   B. time order.

7–10. Complete the outline of the paragraph by finishing the main idea and filling in or completing the major details.

   There are four different _____

   1. _____—for pleasure or enjoyment

   2. Empathic listening—to provide emotional support for the speaker

   3. _____

   4. _____—to evaluate a message to either accept or reject it

RELATIONSHIPS I: Test D

Read each textbook passage, and answer the questions or follow the directions provided.

A. [1]Brainstorming is thinking of as many different suggestions or ideas as possible in a short amount of time. [2]It is a useful way of thinking of creative new ideas and solutions. [3]There are four common guidelines followed by brainstorming groups. [4]First, there must be no criticism of suggestions. [5]Negative evaluations of ideas must be withheld until later. [6]The second guideline is that wild ideas are welcomed. [7]It is easier to tame down an idea than to perk it up. [8]Third, aim for quantity. [9]The greater the number of ideas, the greater the likelihood of winners. [10]The final guideline is that combinations and improvements of ideas are welcomed. [11]In addition to contributing ideas of your own, you should suggest how the ideas of others can be improved or combined.

____ 1. The main pattern of organization of the above selection is
   A. list of items.
   B. time order.

____ 2. Write the number of the sentence that states the main idea of the paragraph.

3. The major supporting details are introduced with the transitions *first, second, third,* and _____.

B. [1]Although few circumstances make us quake 'n' shake as much as speaking in public does, there are some simple ways to cope. [2]For one thing, use visual aids or handouts if possible, to take the focus off you. [3]Slides are an example of a common useful visual aid. [4]Also, have a glass of water handy. [5]This serves two purposes: It's a prop, and it helps keep the mouth moist for easy speaking. [6]Also, stand behind a desk or podium or sit at a table. [7]You'll feel and look more relaxed than if you were "free-standing." [8]Last and perhaps most important, be yourself. [9]Adopting a more formal style will make you, and your audience, less comfortable.

____ 4. The main pattern of organization of the above selection is
   A. list of items.
   B. time order.

5–6. Two of the transitions that signal major details of the paragraph are

_____ and _____.

(Continues on next page)

C. [1]Few products last forever. [2]Most products go through distinct stages of a product life cycle. [3]The first stage in the product life cycle is the introductory stage. [4]During this first phase, the producer tries to stir up demand. [5]Typically, this stage involves expensive advertising and promotion, plus research and development costs. [6]Next comes the growth stage, marked by a rapid jump in sales as the introductory efforts start paying off. [7]As the product enters the growth phase, competition increases, and the war for market share begins. [8]During the third stage, the maturity stage, product sales begin to level off or show a slight decline. [9]The key to success in the maturity phase is to encourage sales of the existing product by broadening its appeal or making minor improvements. [10]Sooner or later most products enter the decline stage. [11]During this last phase, sales and profits begin to slip and eventually fade away.

_____ 7. The main pattern of organization of the above paragraph is
    A. list of items.
    B. time order.

8–10. Complete the map of the paragraph by finishing the main idea heading and filling in the missing major details.

Main idea: There are distinct stages of _____.

Introductory stage: Producer tries to stir up demand; involves expensive advertising and promotion, plus research and development costs

Maturity stage: Sales level off or slightly decline; key to encouraging sales: broaden appeal of product or improve it

RELATIONSHIPS II: Test A

A. Fill in each blank with an appropriate transition from the box. Use each transition once. Then, in the space provided, write the letter of the transition you have chosen.

A. as a result	B. because of	C. differently
D. for example	E. in contrast	

_____ 1. [1]An oldest child is treated _____ in some ways from his or her siblings. [2]For instance, the oldest child is often given the most responsibility, including helping and teaching younger siblings.

_____ 2. [1]In Russia, according to a recent study, only 50 percent of the women and 33 percent of the men said they marry for love. [2]Most said they marry because of loneliness, shared interests, or pregnancy. [3]_____, most Americans (87 percent) say they believe love is essential to a good marriage.

_____ 3. [1]According to the American Cancer Society, one in every twelve Americans is a regular user of chewing tobacco. [2]Many boys feel that it is cool to chew tobacco. [3]However, chewing tobacco contains grit and sand, as well as sugars to improve the taste. [4]_____, it causes tooth decay and tooth loss. [5]In addition, it can cause gum disease. [6]Finally, those who regularly chew tobacco have fifty times the risk of developing cancer than do nonusers.

_____ 4. [1]Chimps and gorillas can communicate with American Sign Language. [2]By learning to make the correct signs with their hands, they can "speak" with humans and others of their species who know the signs. [3]Though the animals have vocabularies of only a few hundred signs, they respond to questions and express wishes. [4]_____, Koko, a signing gorilla in California, asked for (and received) a kitten as a pet.

_____ 5. [1]Chocolate was grown by the Aztecs centuries before the Spanish discovered it in Mexico. [2]It reached Europe, in the form of cocoa, even before coffee and tea did. [3]It spread quickly throughout western Europe. [4]In the late nineteenth century, the Portuguese took the cocoa plant to some islands off Africa. [5]_____ the islands' ideal temperature and humidity, it became an established crop there.

(Continues on next page)

B. Label each passage with the letter of its main pattern of organization. (You may find it helpful to underline the transition or transitions in each item.)

A Definition and example
B Comparison and/or contrast
C Cause and effect

_____ 6. [1]Iced tea, cola, and other drinks that contain caffeine can actually cause you to become overheated. [2]Caffeine causes your blood vessels to become narrower, and narrower blood vessels allow less blood to flow through them. [3]And a weaker blood flow can lead to higher temperatures.

_____ 7. [1]Plea bargaining is the process by which defendants bargain away their right to a trial. [2]The defendants plead guilty to a lesser charge. [3]In return, they receive a lesser punishment than if they were found guilty of the original charge. [4]For example, a person accused of first-degree murder may plead guilty to second-degree murder.

_____ 8. [1]For one study, twenty-six retarded one-year-olds were divided between two types of care. [2]Half were cared for by retarded women. [3]The rest were given routine care in an institution. [4]After three years, the IQ of those mothered by retarded women went up twenty-nine points. [5]In contrast, the babies in institutions lost about twenty-six points. [6]This study suggests that home-like care is much better than institutional care.

_____ 9. [1]The Stockholm Syndrome is the name given to the way some hostages cope: by siding with the people who captured them. [2]The term comes from a 1973 Stockholm, Sweden, bank robbery in which four hostages were held captive for six days. [3]By day six, the hostages had become more loyal to the robbers than to the police. [4]One interesting example of the syndrome is a woman hostage who became attached to one of the robbers involved in her case. [5]In fact, after the incident, she broke her engagement to another man.

_____ 10. [1]Today's teenagers spend billions of dollars on clothing, cosmetics, and other types of products. [2]A few reasons explain why these teens are so interested in buying things. [3]One reason is that today's teens listen to radio and watch TV many hours each week, and they are thus tempted by many advertisements. [4]Another reason is that many teens work numerous hours a week and can afford to buy themselves things.

RELATIONSHIPS II: Test B

Read each paragraph and answer the questions that follow.

A. ¹The story of the city mouse and the country mouse is one version of the age-old debate between the people who prefer city life and those who prefer country life. ²In the city, there is always something to do. ³But in the country, you can always find peace and quiet. ⁴In the city, you are constantly exposed to new and different kinds of people. ⁵On the other hand, in the country you are always among familiar faces. ⁶These are the images we have. ⁷The reality is less clear-cut. ⁸Rural towns do have their night spots, and New York City does have places to escape to and be alone with your thoughts.

____ 1. The main pattern of organization of the selection is
   A. definition and example.
   B. cause and effect.
   C. comparison-contrast.

2. One transition that signals the pattern of organization is _____.

B. ¹A boycott is an organized refusal by people to deal with a person or group in order to reach a certain goal. ²An example is the famous boycott that began in 1955 when Mrs. Rosa Parks of Montgomery, Alabama, refused to obey a law requiring black people to sit at the back of city buses. ³Mrs. Parks was arrested, and her arrest sparked a boycott of the city's bus system by African Americans. ⁴The boycott was organized and led by Dr. Martin Luther King, Jr. ⁵Rather than continue to lose money needed to run the bus system, the city ended the law.

____ 3. The main pattern of organization of the selection is
   A. definition and example.
   B. comparison.
   C. contrast.

4. The word that signals the pattern of organization is _____.

C. ¹Many people say rapid population growth is the reason why nearly one billion people go hungry every day. ²However, political factors are also among the causes of the hunger. ³First, many countries with hungry citizens actually export crops to other countries. ⁴Exporting the crops offers greater profits than selling them at home. ⁵Secondly, surpluses that could feed many people are often destroyed in order to keep the price of products high. ⁶For example, some crops are allowed to rot, and extra milk is fed to pigs or even dumped.

____ 5. The main pattern of organization of the selection is
   A. definition and example.
   B. cause and effect.
   C. comparison-contrast.

6. One word that signals the pattern of organization is _____.

(Continues on next page)

D. [1]The ways athletes deal with their lives after their athletic careers differ greatly. [2]When they are no longer able to perform on the court or the field, some athletes turn to drinking, taking drugs, or other destructive behaviors. [3]However, other athletes plan ahead, taking courses during their peak years and investing their money wisely. [4]For these athletes, life can be very good when the cheering of the fans stops.

___ 7. The main pattern of organization of the selection is
   A. definition and example.
   B. cause and effect.
   C. comparison-contrast.

8. One word that signals the pattern of organization is _____.

E. [1]The "Good Friday" earthquake that occurred in 1964 in Alaska was immensely powerful. [2]In fact, it had effects throughout much of the United States. [3]In faraway Texas, for instance, water sloshed out of swimming pools when the quake hit. [4]In Alaska itself, areas of land were raised and lowered as much as three feet. [5]The shock there caused the tops of trees to snap off. [6]Scientists called the quake one of the most powerful ever recorded. [7]They measured its impact as equivalent to 31.5 million tons of TNT.

___ 9. The main pattern of organization of the selection is
   A. definition and example.
   B. cause and effect.
   C. comparison-contrast.

10. One word that signals the pattern of organization is _____.

RELATIONSHIPS II: Test C

Read each paragraph and answer that questions that follow.

A. ¹Some companies have found that praise can result in improvements in workers' behavior. ²Emery Air Freight provides one such case. ³That company announced the goal of answering all customer inquiries within ninety minutes. ⁴Each customer-service representative was asked to record, on a log sheet, the time it took to answer each call. ⁵If an employee's performance improved, he or she was praised by the supervisor. ⁶Those who didn't improve performance were praised for their honesty and accuracy in filling out their log sheets. ⁷Then they were reminded of the ninety-minute goal. ⁸A few days of such feedback led to impressive results. ⁹Customer-service representatives were meeting the ninety-minute deadline 90 percent of the time.

____ 1. The main idea of the paragraph is expressed in
   A. sentence 1.
   B. sentence 6.
   C. sentence 7.

____ 2. The main pattern of organization of the selection is
   A. definition and example.
   B. cause and effect.
   C. comparison-contrast.

   3. One word that signals the pattern of organization is _____.

B. ¹Positive and negative moods affect our behavior more similarly than you might expect. ²When we are in a good mood, we tend to be more sociable and more giving in our behavior. ³For example, we spend more time with others, and we help others more. ⁴What happens when we're in a bad mood? ⁵You might think that people in a bad mood would be more withdrawn and help other people less, and sometimes this is true. ⁶But often, people who are in a bad mood want to escape that mood. ⁷Instead of acting in a way that is consistent with their bad mood, they try to work themselves out of it by being sociable, by helping others, or by engaging in other positive actions.

____ 4–5. *(Choose two answers.)* This selection has two patterns of organization. It
____ A. defines and gives examples of "positive moods" and "negative moods."
   B. compares positive and negative moods.
   C. discusses the effects of positive and negative moods.

(Continues on next page)

C. [1]Language is appropriate when it is neither too formal nor too informal for the situation. [2]We need to adjust language to the specific person or group we are addressing. [3]Thus, in an interpersonal setting, we are likely to use more informal language when we are talking with our best friend and more formal language when we are talking with our grandparents. [4]In a group or public-speaking setting, we are likely to use more informal language when we are talking with our peers and more formal language when we are talking with strangers. [5]In each of these situations, the differences in our language are appropriate.

___ 6. The selection
- A. defines and illustrates formal and informal language.
- B. discusses the causes and effects of formal and informal language.
- C. contrasts the uses of formal and informal language and the settings in which they are used.

7–10. Complete the chart of the paragraph by filling in the missing details.

Kind of language	_____ setting	Group or Public-Speaking setting
_____ language	_____ _____	When talking with our peers
Formal language	When talking with our grandparents	_____ _____

RELATIONSHIPS II: Test D

Read each paragraph and answer the questions or follow the directions provided. (You may find it helpful to mark the major and minor details as you read.)

A. [1]A common cause of fatigue is physical exhaustion. [2]Such fatigue may be caused by overdoing a difficult physical activity. [3]Waste products build up during physical activity because the body cannot remove them as quickly as they are produced. [4]These waste products cause feelings of fatigue. [5]The fatigue of physical exhaustion is also caused by using muscles that have not been used in a while. [6]Perhaps you have felt such fatigue after trying a new sport for the first time or after buffing wax on a car. [7]A second common cause of fatigue is illness. [8]Poisons from disease-causing agents get into the bloodstream and make you feel weak and tired. [9]You also have less energy when you are ill because the body uses a great deal of energy to fight the infection. [10]A third cause of fatigue is concentrating on mental tasks for a long time without taking a break. [11]Perhaps you have felt extremely tired after studying hard for a test or memorizing lines for a speech. [12]These mental tasks require a great deal of concentration and energy and can cause you to feel tired. [13]A fourth cause of fatigue is strong emotions, which can use up a great deal of mental energy. [14]For example, you might feel exhausted from having an argument with a friend. [15]Finally, boredom is another common experience that causes fatigue. [16]Your energy level can decrease and you can feel very tired just from being bored.

____ 1. The patterns of organization of the paragraph are list of items and
    A. definition and example.
    B. cause and effect.
    C. comparison-contrast.

2–5. Complete the outline of the paragraph by finishing the implied main idea heading and filling in the missing major and minor supporting details.

Main idea: _____ has several causes.

1. Physical exhaustion
    a. From overdoing a difficult physical activity
    b. _____

2. Illness
    a. _____

       _____

    b. Body uses energy to fight infection

3. Concentrating on mental tasks for a long time without taking a break

4. Strong emotions

5. _____

(Continues on next page)

B. [1]In all but the smallest companies, more than one manager is needed to oversee the work of other employees. [2]Companies usually form a management pyramid, with more managers at the bottom than at the top and each level having its own role to play. [3]Top managers set goals and establish policies. [4]An example is the chief executive officer (CEO), who represents the company to the outside world. [5]Middle managers develop plans for carrying out the goals set by top management. [6]Examples are plant managers and division managers. [7]At the bottom of the pyramid are first-line managers, who oversee employees and also put into action the plans developed at higher levels. [8]Positions at this level include foreman, department head, and office manager.

___ 6. The main idea of the selection is expressed in
    A. sentence 2.
    B. sentence 3.
    C. sentence 13.

___ 7. The paragraph
    A. defines and illustrates types of managers in a typical company pyramid.
    B. contrasts types of management pyramids.
    C. explains the effects of various company organizations.

8–10. Complete the map of the paragraph by filling in the missing details.

Management Pyramid

Top managers—have the most power
(*Examples:* Chief executive officer—sets goals, makes long-range plans, establishes policies, represents the company; senior vice president; chairman)

_____
_____
_____
(*Examples*: plant managers, division managers)

_____
_____
_____
(*Examples*: _____)

Name _____

Section _____ Date _____

SCORE: (Number correct) × 10 = _____%

INFERENCES: Test A

After reading each passage, put a check by the **two** inferences that are most firmly based on the given information.

1. [1]Up through the 1700s, many Europeans believed that a king's touch could cure diseases. [2]At his coronation in 1775, for example, King Louis the Sixteenth of France touched 2,400 of his ailing subjects.

   _____ A. The touch of a king truly has special healing power others do not have.

   _____ B. There had been other kings of France named Louis.

   _____ C. French coronations were public events.

   _____ D. The French suffered more illness than other Europeans.

2. [1]Experts have blamed caffeine for bone loss among older women. [2]But a university study of 138 older women found that caffeine had no such effect. [3]In that study, women who drank more than five cups of coffee a day had the same bone density as women who got little caffeine.

   _____ A. Bone loss among older women is not a problem.

   _____ B. The experts who blamed caffeine for bone loss may be wrong.

   _____ C. Caffeine causes healthy bones.

   _____ D. Some older women have experienced bone loss.

3. [1]According to one joke, scientists are now using lawyers instead of rats in laboratory experiments. [2]There are three reasons for this change. [3]For one thing, there are more lawyers than rats. [4]For another, the scientists become less emotionally attached to the lawyers. [5]And finally, certain things are so disgusting that rats won't do them.

   _____ A. A lawyer must have made up this joke.

   _____ B. Some people feel there are too many lawyers.

   _____ C. Lawyers have the reputation of being willing to do anything.

   _____ D. Scientists have the reputation of socializing with lawyers.

(Continues on next page)

4. ^{1}Although lie detector tests are based on a sound principle, they are not always accurate. ^{2}The test is based on the fact that people become emotionally "stirred up" when they lie. ^{3}The lie detector can sense physical changes that accompany such emotional responses. ^{4}But an innocent person may react emotionally to a key question. ^{5}Thus, he or she appears to be lying when actually telling the truth. ^{6}And criminals who lie often may feel no guilt about anything. ^{7}They can therefore tell huge lies without showing the slightest emotional ripple on the lie detector. ^{8}Without an emotional response, there are no physical responses to detect.

_____ A. Criminals never feel any guilt about their crimes.

_____ B. Lie detector tests are not foolproof.

_____ C. Anyone can easily fool the lie-detector machine.

_____ D. An emotional response by an innocent person may register as a lie on a lie detector.

5. ^{1}Eye contact, also referred to as gaze, is how—and how much—we look at people with whom we are communicating. ^{2}Eye contact has several purposes in communication. ^{3}Its presence shows that we are paying attention. ^{4}In addition, how we look at a person reveals a range of emotions such as affection, anger, or fear. ^{5}Moreover, intensity of eye contact may also be used to show dominance. ^{6}For instance, we talk of someone "staring another person down." ^{7}Finally, through our eye contact we can check the effect of our communication. ^{8}By maintaining our eye contact, we can tell when or whether people are paying attention to us, when people are involved in what we are saying, and what their feelings are about what we are saying.

_____ A. Our eyes are more important than our ears in effective communication.

_____ B. Eye contact can be a clue to what we feel and what our listeners feel.

_____ C. Eye contact can never reveal how much power one person has over another.

_____ D. Sometimes a parent can control children just by looking at them.

Name _____

Section _____ Date _____

SCORE: (Number correct) × 10 = _____%

INFERENCES: Test B

A. After reading the passage, put a check by the **two** inferences that are most firmly based on the given information.

1. [1]Two groups of students were gathered as "jurors" in an imaginary court case. [2]One group was told that the defendant was named Carlos Ramirez and that he was from Albuquerque, New Mexico. [3]The other group learned that the defendant was Robert Johnson from Dayton, Ohio. [4]Both groups heard the same evidence against the defendant. [5]When it was time to decide a verdict, the majority of "jurors" found that Ramirez was guilty and that Johnson was innocent.

_____ A. The "court case" was actually an experiment about racial prejudice.

_____ B. The students were Hispanic.

_____ C. The evidence was based upon an actual court case.

_____ D. The experiment revealed the existence of negative stereotypes about Hispanics.

2. [1]The manufacture and sale of alcoholic beverages was outlawed in 1919 by the Eighteenth Amendment. [2]Prohibition, as it was called, achieved a number of good results. [3]It lowered the average consumption of alcohol. [4]Arrests for drunkenness fell sharply. [5]The rate of alcoholism was reduced. [6]If the Prohibitionists had been willing to legalize beer and wine, the experiment might have worked. [7]Instead, by insisting on a totally "dry" society, they drove thousands of ordinary people to break the law.

_____ A. During Prohibition, alcohol was not available.

_____ B. During Prohibition, many usually law-abiding people drank illegally.

_____ C. The Prohibitionists opposed the use of any form of alcoholic beverage.

_____ D. The Prohibitionists were tolerant of moderate social drinking.

(Continues on next page)

B. After reading each short passage, put a check by the **three** inferences that are most firmly based on the given information.

3. [1]Your sister has a new boyfriend. [2]The first time you meet him, he corners you and talks to you for an hour about football, a subject in which you have no interest at all. [3]You come away with the impression that he is an inconsiderate bore. [4]The next two times you see him, however, he says not a word about football. [5]He participates in the general conversation and makes some witty and intelligent remarks. [6]What is your impression of him now? [7]Do you find him likable and interesting on the basis of the last two encounters? [8]Do you average out the early minus and the later plus and come out with a neutral zero? [9]Neither is likely. [10]What is likely is that you still think of him as an inconsiderate bore. [11]Psychological research suggests that first impressions, as our mothers and fathers told us, are quite lasting.

_____ A. The words "neutral zero" refer to an impression that is positive.

_____ B. The words "neutral zero" refer to an impression that is neither positive nor negative.

_____ C. The selection suggests that it's a good idea to make good first impressions.

_____ D. The selection suggests that it can be difficult to remain objective about others.

_____ E. First impressions tend to be fair and balanced impressions.

4. [1]Sociologists distinguish between primary and secondary groups. [2]A primary group is two or more people who enjoy a direct, intimate relationship with one another. [3]We emotionally commit ourselves to a primary group. [4]We view its members— friends, family members, and lovers—as worthwhile and important. [5]They are not simply a means to other ends. [6]A secondary group consists of two or more people who have come together for a specific, practical purpose. [7]The relationship is a means to an end, not an end in itself. [8]Illustrations include our relationships with a clerk in a clothing store and a cashier at a service station.

_____ A. Our secondary groups change more frequently than our primary groups do.

_____ B. It is more difficult to replace a member of a secondary group than a member of a primary group.

_____ C. A favorite teacher is likely to be a member of a student's primary group.

_____ D. It would be difficult to function in society without the aid of secondary group members.

_____ E. Members of our primary group have more power over us emotionally than members of our secondary groups.

INFERENCES: Test C

A. (1–2.) After reading the short passage, put a check by the **two** inferences that are most firmly based on the given information.

[1]Experimenters showed young children one of two short films. [2]In film "A," an adult was shown attacking an inflatable doll. [3]She sat on the toy, punched it in the nose, and threw it about the room. [4]In film "B," the same adult was shown playing quietly with the doll. [5]Later, the children were allowed to play in a room containing many toys, including the inflatable doll. [6]The children who had seen film "A" were much more likely to attack the doll than the children who had seen film "B."

_____ 1. The experiment proved that children are more violent than adults.

_____ 2. The experiment probably was designed to find out if children are influenced by the violence they see.

_____ 3. The results of the experiment suggest that one way children learn to be violent is by seeing violence.

_____ 4. The children who saw film "A" were more violent to begin with.

B. (3–5.) After reading the short passage, put a check by the **three** inferences that are most firmly based on the given information.

[1]Hobbies can serve as promising springboards for business ventures. [2]But to succeed in business, you must balance your creative skills with a knowledge of business techniques. [3]Hobbyists can get the business experience they need in two ways. [4]First, go to work for someone else before going into business for yourself. [5]Consider this first step an apprenticeship in the sort of venture you want to start. [6]Soak up all you can about the problems, the opportunities, and the necessary technical skills. [7]Or you can go directly into business if you have a partner strong in management experience. [8]A hobbyist chef and an experienced restaurant manager may have the right combination of skills to get a venture off the ground.

_____ 1. Being a fine cook is not a good enough qualification for opening a restaurant.

_____ 2. The restaurant business is one of the riskiest ones for a hobbyist to enter.

_____ 3. Creative skills are more important to a business's success than business experience.

_____ 4. Building a successful business requires background in the company's product or service and in business techniques.

_____ 5. A hobbyist chef can get important business experience by working at someone else's restaurant.

(Continues on next page)

C. (6–10.) Read the following textbook passage. Then check the **five** statements which are most logically supported by the information given.

[1]Research has suggested that people are often overly influenced by immediate rewards. [2]Consider a student who has an early morning class in a course in which it is important to attend each lecture. [3]The night before a class, the student decides that a good grade in the course (a delayed reward) is more important than an hour of extra sleep. [4]So he sets his alarm in time to attend the lecture. [5]When the alarm rings the next morning, however, the student changes his mind. [6]Now he chooses extra sleep over a good grade. [7]The immediate reward, extra sleep, now has greater control over his behavior than the delayed reward, a good grade. [8]The power of immediate rewards can be seen in many other situations. [9]Examples are when a person on a diet is confronted with a piece of chocolate cake or when someone trying to save money sees an attractive item in a store window.

[10]Psychologists have developed techniques that dieters, impulsive spenders, and those who tend to oversleep can use when trying to avoid the power of immediate rewards. [11]For example, a student with an early morning class can ask a classmate to stop by on the way to class. [12]That would make it awkward and embarrassing to stay in bed. [13]An impulsive spender may be advised to carry no credit cards and very little cash, making it more difficult to go on a spending spree.

_____ 1. The student who oversleeps generally feels good about his decision to miss class.

_____ 2. Although immediate rewards can be pleasurable, they often interfere with our delayed rewards.

_____ 3. The closer a reward is, the less tempting it becomes.

_____ 4. Since delayed rewards are so hard to achieve, people should avoid them.

_____ 5. To someone trying to quit smoking, a cigarette would be a delayed reward.

_____ 6. To someone on a diet, losing several pounds would be a delayed reward.

_____ 7. Immediate rewards can be more tempting than delayed rewards that are much more important.

_____ 8. Delayed rewards are easier to get than immediate rewards.

_____ 9. Delayed rewards are often of greater long-term value than immediate rewards.

_____ 10. To achieve delayed rewards, it can help to find ways to avoid the temptations of immediate rewards.

INFERENCES: Test D

A. (1–5.) Read the following textbook passage. Then check the **five** statements which are most logically supported by the information given.

¹What would you do if you won ten million dollars in a lottery? ²Your first reaction might be, "I'd spend the rest of my life on the beach (or skiing or traveling)." ³But in all likelihood you, like most other people who receive financial windfalls, would seek some kind of work eventually. ⁴A variety of motives keeps people working, even when they don't need a paycheck to survive. ⁵If you've ever worked as a volunteer, you know that helping someone can be more satisfying than receiving pay. ⁶Work also provides a sense of identity. ⁷One man aged 81 said, "I've been in the fabric business since I was a kid, and I still get a kick out of it."

⁸Studies suggest that rats, pigeons, and children sometimes work to gain rewards, even if they can get the same rewards without working. ⁹One researcher wrote the following on the subject:

¹⁰Rats will run down an alley tripping over hundreds of food pellets to obtain a single, identical pellet in the goal box, . . . and pigeons will peck a key . . . to get exactly the same food that is freely available in a nearby cup. ¹¹Given the choice of receiving marbles merely by waiting a certain amount of time for their delivery, children tend to prefer to press a lever . . . to get the same marbles.

_____ 1. Serving a purpose is satisfying.

_____ 2. It is not so lucky to win a large amount of money in a lottery.

_____ 3. Endless "vacationing" eventually becomes dissatisfying.

_____ 4. The pay we receive is unimportant.

_____ 5. Most people try to work as little as possible.

_____ 6. People, rats, and pigeons enjoy the challenges and interaction that work offers.

_____ 7. It generally feels better to achieve something than to be given something.

_____ 8. People who don't retire continue to work only because they need the money.

_____ 9. Most people who work as volunteers resent the fact that they are not paid for their work.

_____ 10. Work can be its own reward.

(Continues on next page)

B. (6–10.) Read the following textbook passage. Then check the **five** statements which are most logically supported by the information given.

¹In the late nineteenth century, proper heterosexual courtship took the form of "calling." ²When a young woman reached marriageable age, she was allowed to receive male callers in her home, under the watchful eye of a chaperone. ³The entire calling system was controlled by women and took place in their sphere. ⁴A young man was allowed to pay a call only if he was definitely invited by a young woman or her mother. ⁵It was considered highly unsuitable for a man to force his attention on a lady by making the first move.

⁶By the mid-1920s, an entirely new system of courtship—the date—had taken over. ⁷Couples who dated no longer sat together in the front parlor of a private home. ⁸They went out to theaters, restaurants, and dance halls. ⁹This move into the public sphere gave couples unheard-of freedom. ¹⁰It also changed power relations between the sexes. ¹¹Men, who controlled the public sphere, now controlled courtship. ¹²Now women were forbidden to take the first step. ¹³According to mid-twentieth-century advice manuals, girls who refused to respect "the time-honored custom of waiting for boys to take the first step" would ruin a good dating career.

_____ 1. Mothers would definitely have preferred the dating system to the calling system.

_____ 2. Under the system of calling, women saw only those men in whom they or their mothers were genuinely interested.

_____ 3. A nineteenth-century man who showed up uninvited at a woman's home would be considered ill-mannered.

_____ 4. What is considered proper in one generation may be improper in another.

_____ 5. Despite the differences in customs, the same rules of proper behavior continue from generation to generation.

_____ 6. Chaperones were still common in the 1920s.

_____ 7. Parents had less control over dating than they had over calling.

_____ 8. Changes in the rules for courtship take many generations.

_____ 9. It would have been easier for young couples to have sexual relations in the late nineteenth century than in the mid-1920s.

_____ 10. In the late nineteenth century, it could have been difficult for a young man and young woman to be alone.

IMPLIED MAIN IDEAS: Test A

A. In the space provided, write the letter of the general idea that best covers the specific ideas. Remember that the correct general idea will not be too narrow or too broad. It will describe what the specific ideas have in common.

____ 1. *Specific ideas:* horror, shame, disgust, fear

The general idea is
A. emotions.
B. calm emotions.
C. unpleasant emotions.

____ 2. *Specific ideas:* infant, toddler, grade schooler, teenager

The general idea is
A. stages.
B. stages of life.
C. stages of youth.

____ 3. *Specific ideas:* lose weight, quit smoking, cut down on fats, eat more fiber

The general idea is
A. ways to cure illness.
B. ways to become healthier.
C. ways to become richer.

____ 4. *Specific ideas:* mascara, night cream, hair spray, lipstick

The general idea is
A. beauty products.
B. makeup.
C. items bought in a drugstore.

____ 5. *Specific ideas:* California, New York, Georgia, Rhode Island

The general idea is
A. states.
B. large states.
C. northern states.

____ 6. *Specific ideas:* "Ouch, that hurts," "Oh, my aching back," "The children upstairs are too noisy," "My teacher assigns too much work"

The general idea is:
A. complaints.
B. comments.
C. complaints about physical pain.

(Continues on next page)

___ 7. *Specific ideas:* staples, Scotch tape, pens, paper clips

The general idea is

A. office supplies.

B. items for fastening papers.

C. office items that are sharp.

___ 8. *Specific ideas:* "See you," "Bye," "Catch you later," "So long"

The general idea is

A. words of conversation.

B. words of good-bye.

C. words.

B. (9–10.) Each group is made up of four sentences with an unstated main idea. Write the letter of the answer that best states the implied main idea of each group.

Group 1

1. Many college students budget their time poorly and thus often feel anxious about unfinished tasks.
2. Students may feel so much pressure to do well that they work constantly, allowing little time for rest or recreation.
3. Cramped and crowded dormitories can be noisy and unpleasant.
4. Students may feel great pressure to act in certain ways in order to be accepted by a particular group.

___ The unstated main idea of these sentences is:

A. It is important for students to allow sufficient time for rest and relaxation.

B. College can be a very stressful experience.

C. Some college students care more about social acceptance than their own standards.

D. Learning to budget one's time is an essential part of succeeding in college.

Group 2

1. In 1833, Oberlin College became the nation's first coeducational college.

2. In 1837, Mary Lyon established the first women's college, Mount Holyoke, to train teachers and missionaries.

3. Three colleges for blacks were founded before the Civil War.

4. A few other colleges—including Oberlin, Harvard and Dartmouth—admitted small numbers of black students in the nineteenth century.

___ The unstated main idea of these sentences is:

A. In a democracy, a college education should be available to members of all groups.

B. Women could first go to college in the United States in the 1800s.

C. It was in the 1800s that women and African-Americans were first able to go to college in the United States.

D. Several of the nation's colleges are well over 150 years old.

IMPLIED MAIN IDEAS: Test B

A. In the following items, the specific ideas are given, but the general ideas are unstated. Fill in the blanks with the unstated general ideas.

1. *General idea:* _____

   Specific ideas: situation comedy   drama

   soap opera   miniseries

2. *General idea:* _____

   Specific ideas: linoleum   rugs

   carpeting   ceramic tile

3. *General idea:* _____

   Specific ideas: organize coupons   make a list

   look through cupboards   check supermarket ads

4. *General idea:* _____

   Specific ideas: poached   sunny-side up

   scrambled   fried

5. *General idea:* _____

   Specific ideas: do research   prepare outline

   write rough draft   type final copy

6. *General idea:* _____

   Specific ideas: Amen   And they lived happily ever after.

   The End   That's all, folks!

7. *General idea:* _____

   Specific ideas: zebra   candy cane

   tiger   barbershop pole

8. *General idea:* _____

   Specific ideas: snakes   heights

   flying in an airplane   being in small spaces

(Continues on next page)

B. Write the letter of the implied main idea of each of the following two paragraphs.

___ 9. ¹One clue to what a textbook chapter is about is its title. ²Also, the chapter may begin with a short overview—a paragraph or a list of points with a heading such as "Chapter Preview" or "Learning Objectives." ³Opening material like this is your second clue. ⁴It lets you know what major topics will be covered. ⁵For a third type of clue, look at the headings and subheadings within the chapter, to see how the subject matter is organized. ⁶They tell you about relationships among the topics. ⁷Other helpful clues are visual aids: tables, charts, graphs, and photos. ⁸These are usually included to highlight important material. ⁹For further clues, look for key words emphasized in boldface or color. ¹⁰These are vocabulary terms you will need to know.

   A. A textbook chapter contains several elements.
   B. You can learn what a textbook chapter is about by looking at several clues.
   C. Some parts of a textbook chapter are more important than others.
   D. Key words are often emphasized by the use of boldface or color.

___ 10. ¹In the ancient kingdom of Babylonia, a man named Enlil-Bani was chosen to be "king for a day" as part of the New Year's celebration. ²Enlil-Bani was the real king's gardener. ³According to custom, the mock king would rule for a day and then would be killed as a sacrifice to the gods. ⁴In Enlil-Bani's case, however, the real king died during the celebration. ⁵As a result, the lucky gardener remained on the throne for twenty-four years.

   A. Ancient civilizations were extremely brutal.
   B. Babylonians believed in human sacrifices.
   C. A doomed Babylonian gardener became a king by accident.
   D. The Babylonians had a deadly New Year's custom that ended in human sacrifice.

IMPLIED MAIN IDEAS: Test C

Write the letter of the implied main idea in each of the following paragraphs.

____ 1. [1]In his book *Anatomy of an Illness,* writer Norman Cousins described his battle with a severe joint ailment. [2]Told that his doctors could do no more for him, he checked out of the hospital and into a pleasant hotel room. [3]He spent weeks watching Marx Brothers movies and other comedies. [4]He read the funniest authors he could find. He joked and wisecracked with his visitors. [5]Cousins' health improved so much that his doctors were amazed.

    A. Doctors could not do anything to cure Cousins' joint problem.
    B. The Marx Brothers were the stars of movie comedies.
    C. Norman Cousins had a severe joint ailment.
    D. Cousins' experience suggests that laughter may help to heal the body.

____ 2. [1]We're often told "He who hesitates is lost," but we're also warned to "look before you leap." [2]Most of us have heard the saying, "Out of sight, out of mind," but then we hear "Absence makes the heart grow fonder." [3]Everyone talks about "love at first sight." [4]But then someone reminds us, "Marry in haste, repent at leisure." [5]It's all very confusing.

    A. "He who hesitates is lost" seems to be the opposite of "Look before you leap."
    B. Absence does not make the heart grow fonder.
    C. "Love at first sight" is a myth.
    D. Some common sayings seem to contradict each other.

____ 3. [1]Rock, which was first called rock and roll, includes several different styles. [2]All of those styles, however, focus on vocal music—one or more singers—often accompanied by electric guitars. [3]Other common rock instruments are electric instruments, including the bass and drums. [4]All forms of rock feature a hard, pounding, very powerful beat. [5]Another feature is loudness, often so great it can damage players' hearing.

    A. Rock is played by certain characteristic instruments.
    B. The various styles of rock have totally different features.
    C. All styles of rock share certain distinct features.
    D. Electronic instruments help to make rock loud.

(Continues on next page)

_____ 4. ¹At nine months many infants are watching television, though not necessarily understanding it. ²By three or four years of age, they average four hours of TV a day. ³In middle childhood and adolescence, twenty to twenty-five hours a week is about average. ⁴Some youngsters manage a forty-hour week in front of the tube.

    A. Children start to watch television when they are very young.
    B. As children get older, they watch more and more television.
    C. Some children watch television for as much as forty hours a week.
    D. Too much television is bad for children.

_____ 5. ¹Nearly all people at times feel sad and think things are hopeless. ²Depressed by some event or circumstance, they may be unable to perform their normal activities. ³Also, they may have no appetite. ⁴This type of depression affects nearly everyone; as a result, psychiatrists often refer to it as "the common cold of mental illness." ⁵However, for some individuals, depression is a more extreme condition. ⁶This state, called clinical depression, is more lasting and seems to be unrelated to any stressful life event.

    A. There are two types of depression.
    B. Most people feel depressed at times.
    C. Depression is like the common cold.
    D. Clinical depression is a serious illness.

IMPLIED MAIN IDEAS: Test D

Write the letter of the implied main idea in each of the following paragraphs.

___ 1. ¹The first step in answering a multiple-choice item is to read it carefully. ²This will help you see exactly what you are being asked, so that you don't answer the wrong question—an all-too-common mistake. ³Second, think how you would answer the item if *no* choices were given. ⁴If your own answer matches one of the choices, that may be the right one. ⁵Third, look at all the choices. ⁶No matter how sure you may feel, your first reaction might be wrong, so it's a smart idea to consider each option. ⁷Fourth, if you don't know the answer, make an "educated guess" by eliminating any choices that are obviously wrong. ⁸This improves your chance of picking the right choice.

    A. Read a multiple-choice question carefully before you answer it.
    B. There are four steps to follow when you answer multiple-choice questions.
    C. It's all right to guess when you answer multiple-choice questions.
    D. Multiple-choice questions are the most common form of test questions.

___ 2. ¹If you have an automobile accident, stop immediately, but try not to block traffic. ²Keep calm. ³Be polite—don't blame or accuse the other driver. ⁴Help anyone who has been injured, but don't try to move someone who is seriously hurt. ⁵Call the police at once. ⁶When they arrive, answer their questions calmly. ⁷Get, and write down for yourself, the following information about each car and driver involved: name, address, license plate number, make and model of car, insurance company. ⁸Notify your own insurance company as soon as possible, usually within twenty-four hours.

    A. Automobile accidents happen to everyone.
    B. Because accidents happen, you should definitely have automobile insurance.
    C. Here's what you should do if you are involved in an automobile accident.
    D. If you're involved in an automobile accident, call the police immediately.

___ 3. ¹One frequent sleep problem among children is known as "night terrors." ²A child suffering from night terrors will wake up screaming and frightened, but without a memory of any scary dream. ³Another common sleep disturbance, of course, is the nightmare. ⁴Most children occasionally suffer from frightening dreams that make them wake up terrified. ⁵Sleepwalking and talking during sleep are other common childhood problems that interfere with sleep. ⁶Also, some children develop nighttime fears that make getting to sleep difficult, such as the belief that there is a monster hiding under their bed.

    A. "Night terrors" are a frequent sleep problem among children.
    B. Children's sleep problems can be prevented.
    C. Nightmares are the most common form of sleep disturbance.
    D. There are several common sleep problems in childhood.

(Continues on next page)

___ 4. [1]The death of a loved one, especially a husband or wife, is usually ranked as the most stressful event a person can experience. [2]Other experiences that cause great stress are a life-threatening illness and a serious accident or injury. [3]Divorce, loss of a job, and being a victim of crime are also very stressful. [4]But positive events can cause stress too. [5]Examples are a new job (even if it's a better one), marriage, a new baby, and even a vacation trip.

    A. The worst thing that can happen to a person is the death of a loved one.
    B. Serious injuries and life-threatening illnesses are major sources of stress.
    C. Stress can be caused by both positive and negative experiences.
    D. Stress is a normal part of everyone's life.

___ 5. [1]Every ten seconds a home or business somewhere in the United States is broken into, according to police reports. [2]Many houses broken into are unlocked, so the first and most logical protection is to keep doors and windows locked. [3]Another way to protect against burglaries is to have a security system linked to an alarm company that will call the police if a break-in occurs. [4]But the most effective preventive of all against break-ins, according to career criminals, is a large dog.

    A. There are three good ways to protect against burglaries.
    B. The number of burglaries in the United States is increasing.
    C. Locking doors and windows will protect a house from burglary.
    D. Most criminals are afraid of large dogs.

THE BASICS OF ARGUMENT: Test A

A. In each of the following groups, one statement is the point, and the other statements are support for the point. Identify each point with a **P** and each statement of support with an **S**.

Group 1

_____ 1. Ravi arrived at work a half hour late because of a huge traffic jam.

_____ 2. A pen leaked ink on Ravi's new shirt just before he had to go to a meeting with his boss.

_____ 3. Ravi slipped and fell in the middle of the hallway in front of all his coworkers.

_____ 4. Ravi is having a bad day.

Group 2

_____ 5. Millions of bacteria live and breed on human skin.

_____ 6. Tiny mites live in people's hair and on their beds, feeding on dead skin.

_____ 7. The human body is home to many different creatures.

_____ 8. Microscopic worm-like creatures live in the eyelashes of most people, enjoying the warmth and safety of the human eye.

B. (9.) Below is a point followed by three clusters of information. Put a check (✓) next to the **one** cluster that logically supports the point.

Point: This past winter was very severe.

_____ A. [1]The East got its usual amount of snow, and cold air swept over areas from the Midwest to the West Coast. [2]In Minnesota, temperatures were below zero for two weeks, as is usually the case. [3]The South was a bit chilly, but nothing out of the ordinary.

_____ B. [1]In January, heavy snows blanketed most of the country, even areas that rarely see snow. [2]At the end of December, severe flooding caused millions of dollars of damage in several coastal states. [3]Several huge ice storms knocked power out for millions of people this winter. [4]Most agree this was the worst winter in recent memory.

_____ C. [1]Some areas of the Midwest normally have temperatures below zero. [2]However, most of this winter was warm enough for people to wear light jackets. [3]In the Northeast, there was very little snow. [4]And in the South, trees and flowers started their spring growth early because the ground was so warm.

(Continues on next page)

C. (10.) Read the three items of supporting evidence below. Then write the letter of the point that is most logically supported by that evidence.

Support:

> - The mall—with two department stores, various specialty stores, and restaurants—provides one-stop shopping.
> - The mall has plenty of indoor and outdoor parking.
> - Many local seniors like to walk in the new mall because it's safe and air-conditioned.

____ **Point:** Which of the following conclusions is best supported by all the evidence above?

A. Every town needs a mall.
B. The new mall is very convenient.
C. Malls are important to the nation's economy.
D. The mall will find it difficult to compete with a new discount store nearby.

THE BASICS OF ARGUMENT: Test B

A. Each point is followed by three statements that provide logical support and two that do not. In the spaces, write the letters of the **three** logical statements of support.

Point: My next-door neighbors are inconsiderate.
  A. They let their dogs wander around in my yard whenever I am not home.
  B. They pile their garbage next to my fence so that the smell blows into my kitchen window.
  C. The man drives his daughter to school each morning just as I am waking up.
  D. They play loud music in the middle of the night—even on a work night.
  E. He and his wife like to plant flowers in their front yard.

1–3. *Items that logically support the point:* _____ _____ _____

Point: Building a house on beachfront property is a bad idea.
  A. Beachfront properties provide beautiful views for homeowners.
  B. One out of three beachfront homes is damaged or destroyed by storms.
  C. It is very difficult to get insurance for the special problems of beachfront homes.
  D. Ocean levels are expected to rise over the next few years, causing even more damage to beachfront properties.
  E. Some of the most expensive houses in the country are on beachfront land.

4–6. *Items that logically support the point:* _____ _____ _____

Point: A curfew of 9 p.m. should be set for all teenagers.
  A. Teenage drivers cause 75 percent of all accidents that happen after 9 p.m.
  B. Not all teenagers are troublemakers.
  C. Most crimes involving teenagers happen in the evenings.
  D. Many teens have to work at their jobs after 9 p.m.
  E. On average, teenagers who are home during the evenings have higher grades than those who are not.

7–9. *Items that logically support the point:* _____ _____ _____

(Continues on next page)

B. (10.) Below is a point followed by three clusters of information. Put a check next to the **one** cluster that logically supports the point.

Point: Ralph has serious financial problems.

_____ A. [1]He bought a new car this year even though his last car was only three years old. [2]He recently took his girlfriend on an expensive trip to Hawaii. [3]They stayed at a nice hotel and ate all their meals out. [4]While they were there, he proposed marriage to her and gave her an expensive diamond ring he had just bought.

_____ B. [1]All of his credit cards have high balances; one of his accounts has been sent to a collection agency. [2]His rent payment almost equals his monthly salary. [3]And he still owes thousands of dollars in student loans.

_____ C. [1]He has asthma, which makes him cough and wheeze almost daily. [2]In addition, he has bad knees from an old football injury. [3]Last year, his knees became so sore that he stopped exercising and started to gain weight. [4]Today he is so overweight that his doctor is worried about him.

Name _____

Section _____ Date _____

SCORE: (Number correct) × 10 = _____%

THE BASICS OF ARGUMENT: Test C

A. In the following group, one statement is the point, and the other statements are support for the point. Identify the point with a **P** and each statement of support with an **S**.

_____ 1. People who have pets tend to resist diseases better than others.

_____ 2. Studies show that people who own dogs and cats have a lower risk of heart disease.

_____ 3. Pet ownership is healthy for people.

_____ 4. Petting an animal can lower blood pressure by as much as 15 percent.

B. Each point below is followed by three clusters of information. Put a check (✓) next to the **one** cluster that logically supports the point.

5. **Point:** Lena is courteous and kind.

_____ A. [1]Wherever she goes, she asks a lot of questions. [2]She always wants to know what is going on. [3]She reads newspapers, magazines, and books because she wants to learn. [4]In her college classes, her teachers always spend a portion of their class time answering her questions.

_____ B. [1]Whenever she goes to the store, she volunteers to help older people who are loading their cars. [2]If she drives past someone whose car has broken down, she stops and offers to help. [3]And when it snows, she shovels her elderly neighbor's driveway before she does her own.

_____ C. [1]She talks to everyone. [2]If she goes to the supermarket, she ends up getting into a discussion with the cashier or another customer waiting in line. [3]Even though she just moved last month, she already knows many people on her block because she talks to them as they walk by her apartment.

6. **Point:** The house on the corner has a long, interesting history.

_____ A. [1]The paint on the house is faded and flaking off. [2]One of the windows in the attic is missing, and the shingles on the roof are worn and curled. [3]There are small cracks in several of the house's walls, and the curtains in the windows are yellow and torn.

_____ B. [1]Neighbors report hearing noises coming from the house late at night, but no one lives there. [2]An odd black cat sometimes sits on the front step of the house but runs away before anyone can pet it. [3]A few kids said they once saw strange green and blue lights flickering in the second-floor bedroom.

_____ C. [1]The house was built long before the roads were paved. [2]Over a hundred years ago it was used as a post office. [3]Later it became a small general store, selling goods to those who came to pan for gold. [4]Only in the last fifty years was it devoted entirely to being just a house.

(Continues on next page)

C. The point below is followed by three statements that provide logical support and two that do not. In the spaces, write the letters of the **three** logical statements of support.

Point: Being a volunteer can be a very positive experience.
A. Finding time to do volunteer work is difficult, especially for parents of young children.
B. Volunteer work helps people get to know each other better.
C. Doing volunteer work teaches people about the difficulties that others face.
D. By volunteering, many people learn skills that they can use in their jobs.
E. Some volunteer work can only be done by people with special skills.

7–9. *Items that logically support the point:* _____ _____ _____

D. (10.) Read the three items of supporting evidence below. Then write the letter of the point that is most logically supported by that evidence.

Support:

> • Many small movie theaters have closed because they could not compete with the large new multiplexes with many screens.
> • Small corner bookshops have lost the battle with huge new bookstores.
> • Neighborhood hardware stores have been forced out of business by giant "home and garden" warehouse centers.

___ **Point:** Which of the following conclusions is best supported by all the evidence above?
A. People enjoy the personal connection at small, local stores.
B. Bigger bookstores have more books to offer than small bookstores.
C. In recent years, very large stores have forced many small ones out of business.
D. Some small theaters have managed to stay open by charging very low prices for tickets.

THE BASICS OF ARGUMENT: Test D

A. In the following group, one statement is the point, and the other statements are support for the point. Identify the point with a **P** and each statement of support with an **S**.

_____ 1. Undercooked meat may contain worms and parasites that can infect people.

_____ 2. Healthy food preparation requires care in cleaning and cooking.

_____ 3. Unwashed fruits and vegetables are usually coated in chemicals that can be harmful to the body.

_____ 4. Dishes and counters that aren't cleaned properly can spread disease-carrying bacteria.

B. Below is a point followed by three clusters of information. Put a check (✓) next to the **one** cluster that logically supports the point.

5. **Point:** Suburban growth has caused environmental problems throughout the nation.

_____ A. [1]The growth of suburbs has threatened the water supply of several cities, including Phoenix and Las Vegas. [2]In the Northeast, suburban sprawl has greatly reduced the land available for wildlife. [3]And new suburbs in the Midwest have brought air pollution to areas that were once prairies.

_____ B. [1]New housing construction in suburbs provides jobs. [2]It also raises tax dollars and increases property value. [3]In addition, new housing leads to economic growth by creating the need for other kinds of businesses—stores, hospitals, schools, banks, etc.

_____ C. [1]Suburban growth lures jobs and people out of cities. [2]In the Northeast, so many people and businesses have moved to suburbs that the cities have begun to decay. [3]Across the nation, fewer people are left to pay city taxes. [4]As a result, city services often don't have enough money to operate properly.

C. The point below is followed by three statements that provide logical support and two that do not. In the spaces, write the letters of the **three** logical statements of support.

Point: Junk mail should be outlawed.

A. Many companies make millions of dollars worth of sales through their use of junk mail.

B. Each year millions of tons of paper are wasted on junk mail nobody wants.

C. The manufacturing of the ink and paper used to make junk mail contributes to the nation's pollution problems.

D. Some people don't mind receiving junk mail; some even enjoy it.

E. Too much of our precious landfill space is used up by junk mail that is thrown away.

6–8. *Items that logically support the point:*   _____ _____ _____

(Continues on next page)

D. (9–10.) For each group, read the three items of supporting evidence. Then write the letter of the point that is most logically supported by that evidence.

Group 1

Support:

> • The birthrate for women ages 40–44 rose nearly 50 percent over the last twenty years.
> • Since 1970, the percentage of women who had a first child after age 30 increased 400 percent.
> • In the last fifteen years, the birthrate of women in their twenties has declined.

___ **Point:** Which of the following conclusions is best supported by all the evidence above?

    A. Women are having fewer babies today than they used to.
    B. Women shouldn't wait so long to have their babies.
    C. Women today are having their children later in life than they used to.
    D. Teenagers are having fewer and fewer babies each year.

Group 2

Support:

> • Attractive displays are placed at the ends of aisles to get people to buy the products.
> • Necessities such as milk and bread are kept deep in the store so customers must pass many other aisles to get to them—perhaps buying other things along the way.
> • Impulse items, such as candy and magazines, are placed near supermarket check-out lines so people will buy them just before they leave the store.

___ **Point:** Which of the following conclusions is best supported by all the evidence above?

    A. By buying impulse items, people can spend much more than they intended to.
    B. Supermarkets want to help customers use good spending and eating habits.
    C. Supermarkets use special methods to get people to spend more money.
    D. Most of the products sold by supermarkets are overpriced and unhealthy.

Name _____

Section _____ Date _____

SCORE: (Number correct) × 12.5 = _____%

COMBINED SKILLS: Test A

After reading the passage, write the letter of the best answer to each question.

¹The effect of sleep deprivation on your test-taking ability depends on the type of exam questions. ²If they're multiple choice or true/false questions, a night without sleep won't affect your ability to deal with them. ³The reason is that in answering such questions you rely on familiar, established problem-solving techniques. ⁴Such techniques are unaffected by the loss of one night's sleep. ⁵If, however, your exam included essay questions, you'd be in trouble. ⁶To answer this type of question, you need to think flexibly. ⁷And this ability is diminished after only a single sleepless night.

____ 1. In sentence 1, the word *deprivation* means
   A. oversupply.
   B. fear.
   C. loss.
   D. appreciation.

____ 2. In sentence 7, the word *diminished* means
   A. known.
   B. decreased.
   C. strengthened.
   D. defined.

____ 3. The main idea of this passage is expressed in sentence
   A. 1.
   B. 2.
   C. 6.
   D. 7.

____ 4. A night without sleep most affects your ability to answer
   A. multiple choice questions.
   B. true/false questions.
   C. essay questions.

____ 5. Lack of sleep most weakens
   A. memory.
   B. mental flexibility.
   C. familiar problem-solving techniques.

(Continues on next page)

_____ 6. The relationship between sentences 2 and 3 is one of
   A. addition.
   B. time.
   C. cause and effect.
   D. contrast.

_____ 7. The relationship of sentence 5 to sentences 2–4 is one of
   A. addition.
   B. time.
   C. contrast.
   D. illustration.

_____ 8. We can infer from the passage that
   A. teachers should not use essay questions.
   B. too little sleep one night can harm one's health.
   C. students get more sleep than other people.
   D. too little sleep might weaken one's performance at work.

COMBINED SKILLS: Test B

After reading the passage, write the letter of the best answer to each question.

¹One reason for listening is to help others with their problems. ²One type of helpful response, the supporting response, can take several forms. ³Sometimes it involves reassuring: "You've got nothing to worry about—I know you'll do a good job." ⁴In other cases, support comes through comforting: "Don't worry. We all love you." ⁵We can also support people in need by distracting them with humor, kidding, and joking.

⁶Sometimes a person simply needs encouragement, and in these cases a supporting response can be the best thing. ⁷But in many instances this kind of comment isn't helpful at all; in fact, it can even make things worse. ⁸Telling a person who is very upset that everything is all right or joking about what seems like a serious problem can communicate the idea that you don't think the problem is really worth all the fuss. ⁹People might see your comments as a putdown, leaving them feeling worse than before.

_____ 1. In sentence 3, the word *reassuring* means
  A. kidding.
  B. doubting.
  C. listening carefully.
  D. making confident.

_____ 2. The main idea of the first paragraph of the passage is expressed in sentence
  A. 1.
  B. 2.
  C. 3.
  D. 5.

_____ 3. Which sentence best expresses the implied main idea of the second paragraph?
  A. A supporting response can be the best thing in some cases.
  B. Supporting responses are not always helpful.
  C. People often need encouragement.
  D. A supporting response is rarely helpful.

_____ 4. A supporting response can
  A. reassure.
  B. comfort.
  C. entertain.
  D. all of the above.

(Continues on next page)

_____ 5. The relationship of sentence 5 to sentences 3 and 4 is one of
   A. time.
   B. addition.
   C. illustration.
   D. contrast.

_____ 6. The relationship of sentence 7 to sentence 6 is one of
   A. comparison.
   B. contrast.
   C. addition.
   D. an example.

_____ 7. The first paragraph
   A. describes steps in the process of how best to listen to others.
   B. lists forms of supporting responses.
   C. contrasts types of listeners.
   D. narrates a series of events about listening.

_____ 8. The author implies that when trying to be helpful,
   A. we should rarely use humor.
   B. we must make a judgment about how to be helpful in each case.
   C. we can listen without responding.
   D. all of the above.

Name _____

Section _____ Date _____

SCORE: (Number correct) × 12.5 = _____%

COMBINED SKILLS: Test C

After reading the passage, write the letter of the best answer to each question.

[1]Say that you're interested in selling blue jeans in your community. [2]If your rival is selling blue jeans for $28 a pair, you might try attracting business by offering the jeans for $25. [3]The catch, of course, is that you'll get $3 less than your rival does for each pair you sell, and you'll still have to cover the same expenses—buying the jeans from the manufacturer, paying rent on your store, and so forth.

[4]How, then, can you charge less and still make a worthwhile profit? [5]The answer—you hope—is that the lower price will attract more customers. [6]Even though you make less money than your rival does on each pair of jeans, you'll sell more of them and so come out with a good overall profit.

[7]A business owner who can improve efficiency and reduce operating costs may be able to lower prices without settling for a smaller profit per unit. [8]If you are selling blue jeans, for example, you may find that installing a new lighting system cuts the electric bills. [9]You can maintain your profits at a lower selling price and pass the savings along to customers.

[10]Head-on competition like this tends to keep prices down, which is good for the buying public. [11]At the same time, it holds out the promise of great profits to the business that can sell more of its product or service than competitors do.

____ 1. In the first paragraph, the word *rival* means
    A. neighbor.
    B. competitor.
    C. customer.
    D. manufacturer.

____ 2. In sentence 10, the term *head-on* means
    A. unfair.
    B. rare.
    C. useless.
    D. direct.

____ 3. Which subject is the main topic of the passage?
    A. Head-on competition
    B. Blue jeans
    C. Electric bills
    D. Business expenses

(Continues on next page)

_____ 4. Which sentence best expresses the main idea of the passage?
  A. There is great competition in blue jeans sales.
  B. A lower price attracts more customers.
  C. Head-on competition tends to keep prices down for the public while holding out the promise of great profits to business owners.
  D. There are several ways for business owners to keep prices down and still make a worthwhile profit.

_____ 5. To charge less and still make a good profit, business owners can
  A. sell more of a product.
  B. cut costs.
  C. both of the above.

_____ 6. The relationship of sentence 8 to sentence 7 is one of
  A. addition.
  B. time.
  C. illustration.
  D. contrast.

_____ 7. In the context of the passage, competition is a(n)
  A. cause of business decisions.
  B. part of a list of items.
  C. new term being defined.
  D. example.

_____ 8. We might conclude from the passage that *without* competition
  A. the public would benefit from lower prices.
  B. business owners would make lower profits.
  C. business owners would have little reason to lower prices.
  D. there would be more products.

COMBINED SKILLS: Test D

After reading the passage, write the letter of the best answer to each question.

[1]Business ethics is more complicated than it used to be. [2]Back in the "bad old days" around the turn of the century, the prevailing view among industrialists was that business had only one responsibility: to make a profit. [3]Railroad tycoon William Vanderbilt summed up this attitude when he said, "The public be damned. [4]I'm working for the shareholders."

[5]The beginning of the twentieth century was not a good time to be a low-level worker or a careless consumer. [6]For instance, people worked sixty-hour weeks under dreadful conditions for a dollar or two a day. [7]The few bold souls who tried to fight the system faced violence and unemployment. [8]Consumers were not much better off. [9]*Caveat emptor* was the rule of the day—"Let the buyer beware." [10]If you bought a product, you paid the price and took the consequences. [11]There were no consumer groups or government agencies to come to your defense if the product was defective or caused harm. [12]And if you tried to sue the company, chances were you would lose.

[13]These conditions caught the attention of a few crusading journalists known as muckrakers. [14]They used the power of the press to stir up public anger and desire for reform. [15]Largely through their efforts, a number of laws were passed to limit the power of monopolies and to establish safety standards for food and drugs.

____ 1. In sentence 2, the word *prevailing* means
   A. unlikely.
   B. friendly.
   C. illegal.
   D. widely accepted.

____ 2. In sentence 11, the word *defective* means
   A. good.
   B. faulty.
   C. harmful.
   D. old.

____ 3. The main idea of the second paragraph is expressed in sentence
   A. 5.
   B. 6.
   C. 8.
   D. 12.

____ 4. The muckrakers were
   A. consumers.
   B. journalists.
   C. employers.
   D. government agencies.

(Continues on next page)

_____ 5. The author quotes Vanderbilt in order to make clear the turn-of-the-century attitude held by
   A. workers.
   B. heads of industry.
   C. muckrakers.
   D. consumers.

_____ 6. The main pattern of organization of the second paragraph is
   A. contrast.
   B. definition and example.
   C. list of items.
   D. time order.

_____ 7. The relationship of sentence 6 to sentence 5 is one of
   A. addition.
   B. time.
   C. illustration.
   D. contrast.

_____ 8. The author implies that
   A. consumers are better off today than they were at the beginning of the twentieth century.
   B. journalism can greatly influence conditions in this country.
   C. at the beginning of the twentieth century, employers sometimes used force to get their way.
   D. all of the above.

ANSWERS TO THE TESTS IN THE FIRST TEST BANK

DICTIONARY USE: Test A

A. 1–2. easy, earthquake *worm*
   3–4. glide, gloat
   5–6. hide-out, hi-fi
   7–8. rock 'n' roll, roger
   9–10. Thursday, tiddlywinks

B. 11. occupation
   12. cancer
   13. error
   14. military
   15. mystery

C. 16. ten
   17. she
   18. card
   19. up
   20. cure

DICTIONARY USE: Test B

1. mar•ket mär′kĭt
2. stick•up stĭk′ŭp′
3. zip•per zĭp′ər
4. di•min•ish dĭ-mĭn′ĭsh
5. pes•ti•cide pĕs′tĭ-sīd′
6. invention, logic
7. logic
8. invention
9. moonstruck
10. logic, moonstruck

11. noun, verb
12. adj., verb, noun
13. adj., noun, pron.
14. prep., adv., adj.
15. verb, noun, adj.
16. volcanoes
17. families
18. halves
19. teeth
20. mice

DICTIONARY USE: Test C

A. 1. A
   2. B
   3. A
   4. 3
   5. 1
   6. B
   7. B
   8. D
   9. 2
   10. 1

B. 11. season
   12. believable
   13. emergency
   14. governor
   15. indifferent

C. 16. nif•ty nĭf′tē
   17. fru•gal froo′gəl
   18. for•feit fôr′fĭt
   19. feath•er•brain fĕth′ər-brān′
   20. ster•e•o•type stĕr′ē-ə-tīp′

DICTIONARY USE: Test D

A. 1. D
   2. B
   3. D
   4. A
   5. A
   6. A
   7. B
   8. A
   9. B
   10. E

B. 11. heroes
   12. cities
   13. calves
   14. sisters-in-law

C. 15. pär′shəl; having a particular
   16.   liking or fondness for
   17. sănd′băgd; treat severely or
   18.   unjustly
   19. tām;
   20.   not exciting, dull, flat

VOCABULARY IN CONTEXT: Test A

A. 1. Examples: *from China, from India, from Greece, from France;* D
   2. Examples: *washing dishes for hours, flipping burgers day after day;* C
   3. Examples: *suicide, murder;* C

B. 4. overjoyed
   5. ceremonies

C. 6. Antonym: *slow down;* D
   7. Antonym: *deny;* B

D. 8. B
   9. A
   10. A

VOCABULARY IN CONTEXT: Test B

A. 1. Examples: *bad news, an F, a "no";* C
   2. *someone was plotting against him, he was being controlled by something put into his brain;* B

B. 3. twist
   4. strengthen
   5. supporter

C. 6. Antonym: *unnoticeable;* B
   7. Antonym: *simple;* D
   8. Antonym: *expert;* C

D. 9. C
   10. A

VOCABULARY IN CONTEXT: Test C

1. A
2. C
3. D
4. B
5. A

6. C
7. D
8. D
9. B
10. C

VOCABULARY IN CONTEXT: Test D

1. A
2. D
3. D
4. C
5. B

6. B
7. D
8. B
9. B
10. C

MAIN IDEAS: Test A

A. 1. footwear   5. family
    2. flavor   6. emotion
    3. fastener   7. road
    4. entertainer

Items 8–15: Answers will vary. Examples are given.

B. 8. leaking toilet, roaches
    9. train, car
    10. peach, plum
    11. beagle, poodle
    12. Christmas, birthday
    13. Spanish, Italian
    14. what, when
    15. buy a home, own a small business

Items 16–25: Specific ideas may vary; examples are given.

C. 16. punishment, jail term
    17. sweetener, sugar
    18. body of water, ocean
    19. exercise, jogging
    20. chore, taking out garbage
    21. medicine, aspirin
    22. difficult weather, blizzard
    23. wood, pine
    24. seasoning, salt
    25. symptom, fever

MAIN IDEAS: Test B

A. 1. book
    2. flower
    3. bedding
    4. expense
    5. reptile
    6. joint
    7. gas
    8. writer

B.

	Group 1	Group 2	Group 3
3	S	S	P
4	P	S	S
5	S	P	S
6	S	S	S

MAIN IDEAS: Test C

Items 1–6: Specific ideas may vary. Examples are given.

A. 1. fish, salmon   **B.** S
    2. amount, ounce   S
    3. outerwear, overcoat   P
    4. dairy product, cheese   S
    5. furniture, chair
    6. fictional character, Scrooge

C.

Group 1	Group 2		**D.**	
SD	T		19.	B
MI	SD		20.	C
T	SD			
SD	MI			

MAIN IDEAS: Test D

A. 1. T   6. Sentence 1
    2. SD   7. C
    3. SD   8. Sentence 5
    4. MI   9. A
B. 5. B   10. Sentence 3

SUPPORTING DETAILS: Test A

Wording of answers may vary.

A. (1–5.) 1. Provide a stimulating environment.
        2. Focus on the child's strengths.
        4. Set an example in your choices of work or hobbies.
        5. Do not use rigid control.
    5. ways *or* ways in which parents can encourage creativity in children
B. (6–10.) *Heading:* . . . influence people's eating habits.

        Culture   Economics
    9. Another
    10. third

SUPPORTING DETAILS: Test B

Wording of answers may vary slightly.

A. (1–4.) 1. Autocratic leader
        2. Democratic leader—shares authority
        3. "Hands off" leader—takes the role of a consultant
    4. three *or* three broad types of leadership
B. (5–10.)

Special interest groups	Public interest groups—pursue benefits for society
[Examples:] Chambers of commerce, trade associations, labor unions, farm organizations	*Examples:* Consumer protection organizations

    9. One
    10. second

SUPPORTING DETAILS: Test C

Wording of answers may vary.
A. (1–6.) 1. . . . you know about and are interested in.
     2. Prepare well.
        a. Organize your points.
        b. Rehearse your speech several times.
     3. Practice relaxation activities just before
        your speech.
        a. Clear your mind.
B. (7–10.) *Heading:* . . . keep the demands of home
        and job in balance.

Set limits.   List things to   Don't aim
               do in order   for
               of importance.   perfection.

SUPPORTING DETAILS: Test D

Wording of answers may vary.
A. (1–6.) 1. b. . . . multiply and spread.
     2. a. Disease is highly contagious.
     4. Decline stage
        b. Sometimes you can transmit the
           disease to others.
     5. Convalescence
        b. Most diseases are not contagious
           during this stage.
B. (7–10.)

Passive   Aggressive   Assertive
behavior   behavior   behavior
                       |
                   Lash out at those
                   who hurt them.

LOCATIONS OF MAIN IDEAS: Test A

1. 5   4. 2
2. 1   5. 1
3. 2

LOCATIONS OF MAIN IDEAS: Test B

1. 1   4. 1
2. 3   5. 2
3. 6

LOCATIONS OF MAIN IDEAS: Test C

1. 8   4. 1
2. 1   5. 3
3. 1

LOCATIONS OF MAIN IDEAS: Test D

1. 1   4. 6
2. 1   5. 3
3. 3

RELATIONSHIPS I: Test A

A. 1. E later   **B.** 6. One
    2. C First   7. after
    3. D In addition   8. Another
    4. B Another   9. Finally
    5. A after   10. A

RELATIONSHIPS I: Test B

A. 1. B   **B.** 6. A
    2. B   **C.** 7. During
    3. A   8. next
    4. B   9. final
    5. A   10. B

RELATIONSHIPS I: Test C

A. 1. A
    2–3. *Any two of these:* first, second, third
B. 4. B
    5. next
C. 6. A
Wording of outline answers may vary.
7–10. *Heading:* . . . types of listening.
     1. Appreciative listening
     3. Comprehensive listening—to understand
        the message of a speaker
     4. Critical listening

RELATIONSHIPS I: Test D

A. 1. A
    2. 3
    3. final
B. 4. A
    5–6. *Any two of these:* For one thing, Also, Last
C. 7. B
Wording of map answers may vary.
8–10. *Heading:* . . . the product life cycle.
     2. Growth stage: Rapid jump in sales;
        competition increases;
        war for market share begins
     4. Decline stage: Sales and profits slip
        and fade away

RELATIONSHIPS II: Test A

A.
1. C differently
2. E In contrast
3. A As a result
4. D For example
5. B Because of

B.
6. C
7. A
8. B
9. A
10. C

RELATIONSHIPS II: Test B

A.
1. C
2. but *or* on the other hand

B.
3. A
4. example

C.
5. B
6. reason *or* causes

D.
7. C
8. differ *or* however

E.
9. B
10. effects *or* caused

RELATIONSHIPS II: Test C

A.
1. A
2. B
3. result in *or* led to

B. 4–5. B, C

C. 6. C
7–10.

	Interpersonal *setting*
Informal *language*	When talking with our best friend
	When talking with strangers

RELATIONSHIPS II: Test D

A.
1. B

Wording of outline answers may vary slightly.

2–5. *Main idea:* Fatigue . . .
  1. b. From using muscles that have not been used for a while
  2. a. Poisons from disease-causing agents get into the bloodstream
  5. Boredom

B.
6. A
7. A

Wording of map answers may vary.

8–10.
Middle managers—develop plans to carry out top managers' goals
First-line managers—oversee employees; put into action plans developed at higher levels
Examples: foreman, department head, office manager

INFERENCES: Test A

1. B, C
2. B, D
3. B, C
4. B, D
5. B, D

INFERENCES: Test B

1. A, D
2. B, C
3. B, C, D
4. A, D, E

INFERENCES: Test C

A. 2, 3
B. 1, 4, 5
C. 2, 6, 7, 9, 10

INFERENCES: Test D

A. 1, 3, 6, 7, 10
B. 2, 3, 4, 7, 10

IMPLIED MAIN IDEAS: Test A

A. 1. C   6. A
   2. C   7. A
   3. B   8. B
   4. A   **B.** 9. *(Group 1)* B
   5. A   10. *(Group 2)* C

IMPLIED MAIN IDEAS: Test B

Wording of answers may vary.

A. 1. Television shows
   2. Floor coverings
   3. Preparation for grocery shopping
   4. Ways to cook eggs
   5. Steps in writing a paper
   6. Endings
   7. Things with stripes
   8. Things people fear
B. 9. B
   10. C

IMPLIED MAIN IDEAS: Test C

1. D
2. D
3. C
4. B
5. A

IMPLIED MAIN IDEAS: Test D

1. B
2. C
3. D
4. C
5. A

THE BASICS OF ARGUMENT: Test A

A. 1. S   6. S
   2. S   7. P
   3. S   8. S
   4. P   **B.** 9. B
   5. S   **C.** 10. B

THE BASICS OF ARGUMENT: Test B

1–3. A, B, D
4–6. B, C, D
7–9. A, C, E
10. B

THE BASICS OF ARGUMENT: Test C

A. 1. S   6. C
   2. S   7–9. B, C, D
   3. P   10. C
   4. S
B. 5. B

THE BASICS OF ARGUMENT: Test D

A. 1. S   **C.** 6–8. B, C, E
   2. P   **D.** 9. Group 1: C
   3. S   10. Group 2: C
   4. S
B. 5. A

COMBINED SKILLS: Test A

1. C   5. B
2. B   6. C
3. A   7. C
4. C   8. D

COMBINED SKILLS: Test B

1. D   5. B
2. B   6. B
3. B   7. B
4. D   8. B

COMBINED SKILLS: Test C

1. B   5. C
2. D   6. C
3. A   7. A
4. C   8. C

COMBINED SKILLS: Test D

1. D   5. B
2. B   6. C
3. A   7. C
4. B   8. D

DICTIONARY USE: Test 1

In the space provided, write the letter of your answer to each question about the two dictionary entries.

> **lift** (lĭft) *v.* **1.** To carry from a lower to a higher position; raise. **2.** To revoke; to put an end to: *lifted the trade restrictions.* **3.** To raise in rank or condition; uplift: *Your phone call lifted my spirits.* **4.** *Informal.* To steal. —*n.* **1.** The act of raising to a higher position. **2.** The distance which something is raised. **3.** An elevation in spirits: *The good news gave us a lift.* **4.** A ride given in a vehicle.

_____ 1. *Lift* would be found on the dictionary page with which guide words?
   A. lift-off/lighthearted
   B. lifesaver/light
   C. lie/lifetime

_____ 2. In what situation would it *not* be appropriate to use the verb definition 4 of *lift?*
   A. When you are writing e-mail to a friend.
   B. When you are writing a formal essay for English class.
   C. When you are having a conversation with your brother.

_____ 3. In the sentence below, the definition of *lift* that applies is
   A. verb definition 1.
   B. noun definition 2.
   C. noun definition 4.

   Because I was too tired to walk, my cousin gave me a *lift* into town in her truck.

_____ 4. In the sentence below, the definition of *lift* that applies is
   A. verb definition 2.
   B. verb definition 3.
   C. noun definition 4.

   After Faye broke up with her boyfriend, her sister took her out to lunch in an effort to *lift* Faye's spirits.

_____ 5. In the sentence below, the definition of *lift* that applies is
   A. verb definition 1.
   B. verb definition 4.
   C. noun definition 2.

   When I got home, I realized that my wallet had been *lifted* by the man who had "accidentally" stumbled into me on the bus.

(Continues on next page)

scout (skout) *n.* **1.** One sent out to gather information. **2.** A guard. **3.** One who seeks out persons with talent, as in sports or entertainment. **4a.** A Boy Scout. **b.** A Girl Scout. —*v.* **1.** To make an introductory survey or inspection. **2.** To observe and evaluate. —**scout' er** *n.*

_____ 6. *Scout* would be found on the dictionary page with which guide words?
   A. scale/scarlet fever
   B. Scorpio/scream
   C. scuffle/seamy

_____ 7. How many syllables are in the word *scout*?
   A. One
   B. Two
   C. Three

_____ 8. The information in parentheses shows the entry word's
   A. spelling.
   B. part of speech.
   C. pronunciation.

_____ 9. The parts of speech shown for *scout* are
   A. noun and verb.
   B. noun and adjective.
   C. adverb and verb.

_____10. Which definition of *scout* fits the sentence below?
   A. One sent out to gather information
   B. One who seeks out persons with talent, as in sports or entertainment
   C. To make an introductory survey or inspection

   A *scout* was sent to spy on the enemy camp, but he never returned.

DICTIONARY USE: Test 2

Below are ten words with some of their dictionary definitions. A sentence using each word is also given. In the space provided, write the letter of the definition that best fits each sentence.

_____ 1. **alter**
   A. To change or make different
   B. To adjust (a garment) for a better fit

   Alcohol *alters* my father's personality.

_____ 2. **depress**
   A. To make sad
   B. To press down; lower
   C. To lower or lessen in value or price

   The rats soon learned that if they *depressed* the button, they would get a treat.

_____ 3. **tender**
   A. Sensitive or sore
   B. Gentle and loving

   I cut my finger last week while trying to slice a bagel, and the cut is still *tender*.

_____ 4. **lonely**
   A. Sad at being alone
   B. Without companions
   C. Empty of people

   Behind the old church was a dark, *lonely* road, which no one dared use anymore.

_____ 5. **illuminate**
   A. To provide or brighten with light
   B. To make understandable; clarify

   Our English teacher is very good at *illuminating* difficult poetry passages.

_____ 6. **observe**
   A. To notice
   B. To make a systematic or scientific observation of
   C. To say by way of comment or remark

   "One of the striking differences between a cat and a lie," *observed* Mark Twain, "is that a cat has only nine lives."

(Continues on next page)

_____ 7. **fade**

    A. To lose or cause to lose brightness or brilliance; dim

    B. To disappear gradually; vanish

    C. To lose freshness; wither

       The coat, which had once been bright red, was _faded_ and torn from years of hard use.

_____ 8. **reflect**

    A. To throw or bend back (light, for example) from a surface

    B. To make apparent; express

    C. To think quietly and calmly

       The more Earl _reflected_ on his arguments with his mother, the more he wished he could change the way he had acted.

_____ 9. **make-up**

    A. The way in which something is arranged or constructed

    B. The mental, physical, or moral qualities that constitute a personality

    C. Cosmetics applied especially to the face

       Honesty is so central to Vic's _make-up_ that cheating is out of the question for him.

_____ 10. **vital**

    A. Essential for the continuation of life

    B. Full of life; energetic

    C. Of great importance; essential

       "It is _vital_ that we create enough parking spaces for the new shopping district to be a success," the mayor insisted.

VOCABULARY IN CONTEXT: Test 1

Use context clues to choose the word closest in meaning to each capitalized word. Then write the letter of your choice.

_____ 1. The closer two people feel, the more likely they are to DISCLOSE private information about themselves.
  A. hide
  B. find
  C. reveal
  D. improve

_____ 2. URBAN residents are victims of crime more often than people who live in the country.
  A. male
  B. female
  C. rich
  D. city

_____ 3. Lea said she failed the test because of trick questions and unfair scoring. She couldn't admit that her grade was a CONSEQUENCE of her lack of study.
  A. cause
  B. surprise
  C. result
  D. delay

_____ 4. Our new house has AMPLE room for a growing family—which is fortunate, since we plan to have at least six children.
  A. too little
  B. unclear
  C. enough
  D. distant

_____ 5. "Don't assume that spelling is a TRIVIAL matter you can ignore," the instructor warned. "In fact, it is very important. Your paper will lose points for misspelled words."
  A. pleasant
  B. major
  C. final
  D. unimportant

_____ 6. Representatives of the union and the company worked far into the night, trying to AVERT a strike. But their efforts failed, and the workers went on strike the next morning.
  A. avoid
  B. continue
  C. describe
  D. start

_____ 7. I worked in the garden last evening until the light had DIMINISHED so greatly that I could hardly see what I was doing.
  A. grown
  B. lessened
  C. encouraged
  D. burst

_____ 8. The SEQUENCE of events in the movie is unusual. The hero's death is shown at the beginning and is then followed by everything that led up to that death.
  A. order
  B. size
  C. length
  D. contents

(Continues on next page)

_____ 9. The DIMENSIONS of a room can affect how people react to it. For instance, if the height of the ceiling is too great, they may feel dwarfed.
- A. location
- B. measurements
- C. light sources
- D. colors

_____10. To avoid being a victim of fraud or false advertising, be SKEPTICAL. Remember, if a claim sounds too good to be true, it probably is not true.
- A. stingy
- B. trusting
- C. honest
- D. doubting

VOCABULARY IN CONTEXT: Test 2

Use context clues to choose the word closest in meaning to each capitalized word. Then write the letter of your choice.

____ 1. The Chinese saying "Talk does not cook rice" IMPLIES that words are sometimes not enough; action is also needed.
    A. hides
    B. asks
    C. denies
    D. suggests

____ 2. To keep the old bridge from falling down, engineers REINFORCED it with steel beams.
    A. reduced
    B. understood
    C. strengthened
    D. measured

____ 3. When Kyle entered the classroom thirty minutes late, the instructor said, "Sir, if you will try to get to class on time in the future, I will ENDEAVOR to pass you."
    A. forget
    B. notice
    C. try
    D. refuse

____ 4. Living things ADAPT to their environment in many ways. Animals may develop thick fur to protect against the cold and wet; plants may grow thorns to keep enemies away.
    A. adjust
    B. leave
    C. arrive
    D. give

____ 5. Tara and her "best friend," Aisha, have an ERRATIC relationship. One day, they are on the phone for hours, and the next, they aren't speaking to each other.
    A. boring
    B. not consistent
    C. regular
    D. new

____ 6. Jurors must be IMPARTIAL in considering evidence. They should not come to a conclusion until both sides are fully heard.
    A. open-minded
    B. prompt
    C. citizens
    D. friendly

____ 7. In public speaking, it is important to be AUDIBLE, but a surprising number of speakers forget this obvious fact and pitch their voices too low for the audience to hear.
    A. able to be heard
    B. interesting
    C. able to be believed
    D. well-informed

____ 8. There has been a long-term debate over whether intelligence is INNATE or developed through experience. Today most psychologists feel it is both.
    A. measurable by IQ tests
    B. possessed at birth
    C. important
    D. learned

(Continues on next page)

_____ 9. Many of the "stars" we see in the sky are ILLUSIONS; the stars are not really there. They died long ago, but their light is still traveling toward us.
  A. misleading images   C. dangers
  B. real objects   D. things that please

_____10. Smart consumers know how to spot DECEPTIVE advertising. They look for misleading wording and false claims, and they read the "small print" they're not expected to notice.
  A. humorous   C. intended to fool
  B. on television and radio   D. reasonable

Name _____

Section _____ Date _____

SCORE: (Number correct) × 10 = _____%

MAIN IDEAS: Test 1

Each group below is made up of four specific ideas and the general idea they belong to. Underline the general idea in each group.

1. Europeans	French	Spanish	Italians	Swiss
2. gravel	concrete	road surface	tar	dirt
3. pole vault	mile run	track and field event	shot put	high jump
4. wallpaper	paneling	ceramic tiles	paint	wall coverings
5. salmon	fish	trout	sardine	tuna
6. gin rummy	Monopoly	baseball	game	chess
7. exclamation point	period	comma	punctuation mark	colon
8. helicopter	aircraft	jetliner	sea plane	glider
9. home	duplex	condo	cottage	apartment
10. surprise quiz	traffic jam	being laid off	misfortune	food poisoning

(Continues on next page)

MAIN IDEAS: Test 2

Each of the following groups of statements includes one main idea and two supporting details. In the space provided, write the letter of each main idea.

_____ *Group 1*

    A. It takes quite a few animals to make an average fur coat.
    B. A mink coat is made from the skins of thirty-five to sixty-five mink.
    C. It takes as many as a hundred animals to make a chinchilla fur coat.

_____ *Group 2*

    A. Before a major stroke, some people experience double vision.
    B. Some people feel temporary numbness in the face, arms or legs before a stroke.
    C. Before a major stroke, the body often sends warnings.

_____ *Group 3*

    A. The largest continent is Asia, which includes about 17 million square miles.
    B. There's a big difference between the largest and the smallest continent.
    C. Australia, the smallest continent, is made up of about 3 million square miles.

_____ *Group 4*

    A. Retro running is less stressful to certain injuries than jogging.
    B. Retro running, which is running backwards, offers advantages to joggers.
    C. Retro running offers joggers a change of pace.

_____ *Group 5*

    A. Takeout foods are convenient for working couples.
    B. Takeout foods are popular with families for two main reasons.
    C. Each member of a family can have what he or she wants for dinner.

_____ *Group 6*

    A. Randell tries to make the most of his college education.
    B. Randell studies for hours every evening with his girlfriend.
    C. Whenever he doesn't understand something, Randell asks the teacher to explain it again.

_____ *Group 7*

    A. It takes forty-three muscles to frown.
    B. Smiling is easier on the face than frowning.
    C. Smiling requires only seventeen muscles.

(Continues on next page)

_____ *Group 8*

A. One city sponsored a dance for which the admission "ticket" was a pair of shoes for the homeless.
B. Communities across the country are finding imaginative ways to help the homeless.
C. One town offered a free dance to the high school that donated the most canned goods to the homeless.

_____ *Group 9*

A. When Jeff was five, he could play any tune he heard on the radio on his toy piano.
B. Jeff learned to play the real piano so quickly that he was able to accompany his elementary-school choir at concerts.
C. It was clear when Jeff was young that he would be a good musician.

_____ *Group 10*

A. The roots of plants have certain functions.
B. Plants take in water and nutrients through their roots.
C. Roots hold plants firmly to the ground, where the plants receive nourishment.

SUPPORTING DETAILS: Test 1

The main idea in each of the following paragraphs is boldfaced. In the space provided, write the number of major details in each paragraph.

_____ 1. [1]Today's teenagers spend billions of dollars on clothing, cosmetics, and other types of products. [2]**Some reasons explain why these teens are so interested in buying things.** [3]One reason is that today's teens listen to radio and watch TV many hours each week, and they are thus tempted by many advertisements. [4]Another reason is that many teens work numerous hours a week and can afford to buy themselves things.

_____ 2. [1]**Psychologists offer reasons to explain why some women marry prisoners they didn't know until they wrote to them in prison.** [2]One reason might be that these women feel somehow safer with their men locked up. [3]Another reason may be that relationships in the "real" world involve day-to-day demands and problems. [4]Some women may find a "fantasy" relationship easier to deal with than a real relationship.

_____ 3. [1]**The shape of a bird's beak is a major influence on what the bird eats.** [2]One type of hummingbird, for instance, has a five-inch bill, enabling it to sip nectar from deep flowers. [3]The cockatoo has a hooked beak, which it uses to crack nuts. [4]And the flamingo has a comb-like edge to its beak. It runs that edge through the mud to sieve out tiny plants and animals to eat.

_____ 4. [1]**People in certain occupations are influenced by how their work is described in fiction.** [2]Private detectives, for example, often use the private eyes in novels as role models for how they should behave. [3]And at Central Intelligence Agency headquarters, experts read spy thrillers for tips that they can apply to real intelligence operations.

_____ 5. [1]Misinterpretations can be expected when translating from one language to another. [2]But they are far too common when someone is speaking our own language. [3]**However, there are ways to avoid misinterpreting what others are saying.** [4]First, listen very closely and carefully to what a speaker is saying. [5]It is also helpful to repeat in your own words what you have just heard. [6]This gives the speaker a chance to clarify any points you might have misunderstood. [7]Finally, ask questions whenever in doubt.

(Continues on next page)

_____ 6. [1]When it's cold outside, homeless people face the challenge of finding a warm, dry place for the night. [2]**One imaginative place to stay overnight is the subway, which meets several needs of the homeless.** [3]First of all, the subway is inexpensive. [4]For about a dollar, a person can travel all night long. [5]Also, the subway is heated, making it a nice warm place to spend the night. [6]Finally, traveling the subway at night is legal, because as long as passengers pay the fare, they need not prove they have a destination.

_____ 7. [1]**There are several types of crime.** [2]The type people fear the most is crimes of violence against people, including, of course, murder and rape. [3]The second type is crimes against property, in which a criminal damages or steals something belonging to another person. [4]Next are crimes without victims. [5]Those who suffer from these crimes are the criminals themselves, including gamblers and prostitutes. [6]Finally, there's white-collar crime, crime committed on the job by respected people in responsible positions.

_____ 8. [1]**Products can be divided into major categories.** [2]The first category is consumer products. [3]They are goods and services purchased by consumers for their own use. [4]Most of the products you buy, including clothing, shampoo, and CDs, are consumer goods. [5]The second category is business products, sometimes called organization or industrial products. [6]These are goods and services purchased for use in the production of other goods for resale. [7]The plastic that Epson buys to build its printers is an industrial product.

_____ 9. [1]Some of the best material for your speech will come from what you read. [2]**There are a few types of written materials that you should consider when preparing a speech.** [3]First, consider books. [4]By checking the card catalog of your library, you are likely to find at least one or two books on your topic. [5]Magazines are also a good resource. [6]You can discover helpful articles by checking the index of magazine articles at the library. [7]Newspapers can also be useful sources of information.

_____ 10. [1]**The ways parents raise their children can be divided into just a few general methods.** [2]Those who set up very strict rules for their children and never explain those rules are using an authoritarian approach. [3]In an authoritarian home, force and punishments are used to make sure children follow rules, and children are given no choices. [4]In contrast, parents who use the permissive approach have few rules. [5]Permissive parents allow children to make their own choices about almost everything, including when they eat and go to bed. [6]In between these two extreme methods of child rearing is the democratic approach. [7]Democratic parents present their children with rules, but they explain the rules to the children. [8]If a child in a democratic home can give a good reason for not following a rule, an exception may be made.

SUPPORTING DETAILS: Test 2

Read each paragraph below, and then write the letter of the correct answer to each question that follows.

A. [1]Small businesses play important roles in our economy. [2]First of all, they create many jobs for Americans. [3]Almost all new jobs created in the United States in the past decade are in businesses with fewer than a hundred employees. [4]Another important way small businesses contribute to our economy is by encouraging new products. [5]Among the products that small businesses have contributed are the safety razor and stainless steel. [6]Third, many small businesses meet consumers' special needs. [7]If you want to rent a Santa Claus suit or buy an odd piece of sheet music, you naturally turn to a small business for help.

____ 1. The paragraph lists
   A. kinds of small businesses.
   B. roles of small business in our economy.
   C. many types of jobs for Americans.

____ 2. The major details of the paragraph are
   A. creating new jobs; encouraging new products; meeting consumers' special needs.
   B. more than a hundred employees; fewer than a hundred employees.
   C. the safety razor; stainless steel.

____ 3. The second major detail is introduced with the word
   A. *another.*
   B. *among.*
   C. *also.*

____ 4. One sentence that provides a major detail is
   A. sentence 2.
   B. sentence 5.
   C. sentence 7.

____ 5. One sentence that provides minor details is
   A. sentence 1.
   B. sentence 5.
   C. sentence 6.

(Continues on next page)

B. [1]According to psychologists, close relationships share a few basic characteristics. [2]First, they usually involve frequent interaction over a long period of time. [3]Second, they include many different kinds of activities or events. [4]For example, friends tend to discuss many different topics. [5]In contrast, shallow relationships may focus on a single activity. [6]The exchanges between a homeowner and the local mail carrier are an example. [7]Last, in close relationships, the influence between people is strong. [8]We may quickly forget a nasty remark from a salesclerk. [9]But we may suffer for weeks about a comment made by our best friend.

___ 6. The words that show that a list is coming are
   A. *psychologists.*
   B. *a few basic characteristics.*
   C. *frequent interaction.*

___ 7. The number of major details listed is
   A. three.
   B. four.
   C. five.

___ 8. The final major detail is signaled with the word(s)
   A. *such as.*
   B. *finally.*
   C. *last.*

___ 9. A sentence that provides a major detail is
   A. sentence 3.
   B. sentence 4.
   C. sentence 5.

___10.   A sentence that provides a minor detail is
   A. sentence 1.
   B. sentence 7.
   C. sentence 9.

LOCATIONS OF MAIN IDEAS: Test 1

In the space provided, write the number of the sentence that expresses the main idea in each paragraph.

_____ 1. ^{1}What makes a marriage happy or unhappy? ^{2}According to psychologists, certain personal qualities can strongly influence how happy people are with their marriages. ^{3}Men and women with self-confidence are more likely than others to be happily married. ^{4}Their spouses are likely to be happy too. ^{5}On the other hand, people who are unstable emotionally are more likely to be unhappily married.

_____ 2. ^{1}In much the same way that humans use creams and lotions to condition their skin, birds use a special oil to condition and waterproof their feathers. ^{2}This oil is a waxy substance contained in an oil gland beneath some feathers on the bird's back. ^{3}After bathing, the bird takes some oil from the gland and smears it over the feathers.

_____ 3. ^{1}When inventor Elias Howe was struggling to invent the sewing machine, he met with little success. ^{2}Then one night he dreamed that a savage tribe had captured him and threatened to kill him if he didn't come up with a working sewing machine quickly. ^{3}When the time was up, his captors threw their spears at him. ^{4}Just before the spears hit him, he noticed that they had eye-shaped holes near their tips. ^{5}He woke up realizing what had been missing in his machine design. ^{6}He quickly made a sewing machine needle with a hole at its point, rather than near the middle or top. ^{7}Thanks to a dream, Elias Howe's sewing machine became a reality.

_____ 4. ^{1}Severe winter storms can be dramatic, beautiful—and inconvenient. ^{2}However, some elementary precautions can reduce the discomfort a storm can cause. ^{3}A storm can disrupt electrical service, causing electric heat to shut down. ^{4}So having a wood stove or fireplace available is a good idea. ^{5}Also, for those times when snow blocks the roads, a supply of canned goods—and a manual can opener—can come in very handy.

_____ 5. ^{1}Because sleep involves a third of the average person's day, it is important in everyone's life. ^{2}Our daily routines revolve around being awake and being asleep. ^{3}Yet people's sleeping patterns vary quite a bit. ^{4}Some adults can function well on four or five hours of sleep. ^{5}Others require nine to ten hours, and the great majority need seven to eight hours of sleep per night. ^{6}Similarly, some people like to go to bed early and rise early, while others are "night owls" who go to bed late and get up late.

(Continues on next page)

_____ 6. [1]Young people may prepare for their future by taking a variety of part-time jobs to test their interest in different fields. [2]Also, they may work very hard on a particular talent such as music, dancing, or art. [3]They might talk with their parents and other adults about jobs and careers. [4]And they might participate in school activities and clubs built around specific interests, such as writing, tutoring, and community service. [5]These are all useful ways for young people to consider which field they would like to work in as adults.

_____ 7. [1]Herbal teas are generally thought to be wholesome. [2]Some herbs, however, have medicinal properties that can be dangerous. [3]For example, the flowers used to make chamomile tea are closely related to ragweed. [4]People allergic to ragweed can suffer serious reactions to chamomile tea. [5]The same is true for goldenrod, marigold and yarrow teas—all available in health-food shops. [6]Also, licorice root, the basis of another herbal tea, can worsen high blood pressure by causing the body to hold sodium and water.

_____ 8. [1]One of the largest international health services is the World Health Organization (WHO). [2]It is a special agency of the United Nations. [3]WHO works to improve the physical and mental health of the world's people in various ways. [4]It spreads new medical and health information to all countries. [5]It provides financial and technical help to control diseases within a country. [6]It also helps prevent diseases from spreading from one country to another. [7]WHO gives emergency help to countries handling epidemics and such special health problems as the care of refugees. [8]Another major activity of WHO is to help people learn good ways to fight water and air pollution.

_____ 9. [1]Do you attend a large or small school? [2]Your answer will depend on what you compare it with. [3]Alongside a campus such as the University of Michigan, with over thirty thousand students, your school may look small. [4]But compared with a smaller institution, it may seem quite large. [5]Similarly, whether or not someone is a fast or slow runner depends on who you compare the person to. [6]Relative words, such as "fast" and "slow," "large" and "small," and "short" and "long," are clearly defined only through comparison.

_____ 10. [1]The negative effects of air pollution on people's health are well known. [2]But there are also great financial costs of air pollution. [3]In New York City, more than $100 million in repainting is required each year because of pollution. [4]Also, since cloth disintegrates and dyes fade faster in polluted air, hotels must wash and replace their curtains frequently. [5]Museums must deal with the pollution that creeps through windows and damages varnish on paintings, blackens bronze objects, and tarnishes ancient jewels. [6]Finally, valuable paper records are damaged by pollution, so expensive microfilming is required.

LOCATIONS OF MAIN IDEAS: Test 2

In the space provided, write the number of the sentence that expresses the main idea in each paragraph.

_____ 1. [1]While a great deal of money has been spent trying to locate the Loch Ness monster in Scotland, many believe "Nessie" to be a myth. [2]Yet it was not so long ago that many animals we have seen and photographed were believed to live only in legends. [3]People once laughed at the idea of large, hairy man-like beings that lived in the plains of Africa. [4]Today we know that gorillas do exist. [5]Many also doubted the existence of the octopus, a creature we're well acquainted with now.

_____ 2. [1]Studies of free-living rats indicate that rat societies are based on cooperation. [2]For example, two rats have been filmed working together to haul an egg back to their colony. [3]While one rat grasped the egg with all four feet, the other pulled the first rat along by its tail. [4]If a mother rat with infants dies, other female rats in the community adopt the infants and raise them as their own. [5]Rats often help provide care for their younger brothers and sisters. [6]They also take care of their parents and grandparents when these older rats become too weak to find food.

_____ 3. [1]Everyone is aware that hypnosis is used to entertain. [2]Under the "spell" of a hypnotist, for example, a subject might bark like a dog for an audience. [3]However, there is a serious use for hypnosis—as a medical tool. [4]When patients with eczema are told under hypnosis that their skin is clearing up, the condition actually improves. [5]Even warts can be eliminated through hypnosis. [6]Headache sufferers also benefit when given suggestions that their tension headaches will no longer occur.

_____ 4. [1]A former rancher is protecting many rare and endangered Hawaiian plants and is working hard to protect even more. [2]About eighty different native Hawaiian plants now grow in his wildlife preserve. [3]They include plants so rare that they are down to their last few individuals in the wild. [4]To make room for more rare plants, he chops down acres of his own trees. [5]Then he burns whatever is left of the trees and sprays to kill any growing thing that remains, creating a home where rare plants will have no competition from other plants.

_____ 5. [1]The teen crowd is the largest and least personal of adolescent groups. [2]Members of the crowd meet because they have a common interest in an activity, not because they are interested in each other. [3]Another adolescent group, the clique, is smaller and involves greater intimacy among members. [4]The most intimate and often the most fulfilling relationships are individual friendships. [5]In general, peer group relationships in adolescence fall into one of the above three categories.

(Continues on next page)

_____ 6. ¹For many of our ancestors, housework was hard physical work. ²Clothing had to be washed by hand and hung up to dry. ³Wood to heat their homes had to be chopped. ⁴Shopping trips may have meant long walks to town. ⁵Today many labor-saving devices have made chores much easier for us than for our ancestors. ⁶We have washing machines, dryers, and dishwashers. ⁷Our homes are heated by machines that need little help from us. ⁸And we can drive a car instead of walking—and put things in the trunk instead of carrying them.

_____ 7. ¹Sherlock Holmes once said he did not believe in ghosts. ²But Sir Arthur Conan Doyle, his creator, was fooled into believing in fairies. ³In 1917, two girls aged 10 and 16 took pictures of themselves playing with fairies. ⁴They claimed the fairies were real. ⁵Doyle believed the photos and the two sisters, who for years stuck by their story. ⁶The girls finally confessed in 1983, when one was 76 and the other 82. ⁷They explained that the fairies were actually stiff paper cutouts propped up with hairpins. ⁸Doyle died in 1930, still believing in fairies.

_____ 8. ¹In the East, World Series games begin at 8:30 p.m. ²Loyal fans must often suffer sub-freezing temperatures and getting home and into bed very late. ³Furthermore, cold fall weather can have a major harmful influence on the quality of play. ⁴In the West, the games begin at 5:30 p.m. ⁵This means fighting rush-hour traffic to reach the game. ⁶West Coast fans thus often arrive at their seats long after the start of the game. ⁷For these reasons, it would be in the best interests of baseball to move the World Series to the daytime.

_____ 9. ¹When approached with another's problem, a common tendency is to try to help by offering a solution. ²Offering advice, however, is often not as helpful as you might think. ³First of all, your suggestion may not offer the best course to follow, in which case it can even be harmful. ⁴There's often a temptation to tell others how we would behave in their place, but what's right for one person may not be right for another. ⁵Also, advice often allows others to avoid responsibility for their decision. ⁶A person who follows a suggestion of yours that doesn't work out can always pin the blame on you. ⁷Finally, often people simply don't want advice. ⁸They may not be ready to accept it, needing instead to talk out their thoughts and feelings.

_____ 10. ¹When digital watches and clocks became inexpensive and common in the 1970s, it looked like the end of the traditional way of telling time. ²Teachers found students who couldn't even tell time from a clock dial, since all they'd seen at home were digital clocks. ³The Swiss watch industry nearly went out of business. ⁴But the truth seems to be that many people feel awkward saying, "It's 6:53" instead of "It's a little before seven." ⁵And to many of us, the moving hand of a clock or watch is still the symbol of passing time. ⁶Thus traditional watches made a comeback. ⁷Despite the appeal of digital watches, the traditional watch has not become a thing of the past.

RELATIONSHIPS I: Test 1

Read each item, and then answer the question about relationships in the space provided. Write in either the transition or the pattern of organization.

1. After I had looked all over the house for my car keys, I found them in the pocket of my other coat.

   The time transition used is _____ *(write one word).*

2. [1]According to a Gallup poll, the most hated household task is washing the dishes. [2]Another despised chore is cleaning the bathroom.

   The addition transition used is _____ *(write one word).*

3. Franklin D. Roosevelt was thirty-nine when he was stricken with polio.

   The time transition used is _____ *(write one word).*

4. [1]In 1926, Gertrude Ederle became the first woman to swim across the English Channel. [2]Furthermore, in doing so she broke the existing men's record.

   The addition transition used is _____ *(write one word).*

5. [1]There are several reasons for the great popularity of professional wrestling. [2]First of all, people enjoy watching all the drama of the "good guy" versus the "bad guy."

   The addition transition used is _____ *(write three words).*

6. [1]Businesses are financed in several ways. [2]Most begin with the founder's personal money. [3]The second most common source of funds is bank loans. [4]Wealthy individuals who wish to invest in new companies are yet another source of funds.

   The selection's main pattern of organization is _____ *(write **list** or **time**).*

7. [1]There is often a series of steps in the hiring process. [2]First of all, a small number of qualified candidates are selected from the total number of people who applied. [3]The next step is to interview each candidate to clarify his or her qualifications and to fill in any missing information. [4]The third step is sometimes a test or a series of tests.

   The selection's main pattern of organization is _____ *(write **list** or **time**).*

8. [1]Air usually enters your respiratory system through your nostrils. [2]It then passes into the nasal cavity, a space between the nostrils and throat. [3]Next, the air travels from the nasal cavity into the passageway called the pharynx. [4]From the pharynx, air travels through a short passageway called the larynx, where your vocal cords are located.

   The selection's main pattern of organization is _____ *(write **list** or **time**).*

(Continues on next page)

9. ¹During the Depression, the nation's banks were closed for a week, and many people turned to barter to pay for things. ²One truck driver was stopped for a traffic violation in Stuttgart, Arkansas. ³He paid his fine with two bags of rice. ⁴Barter was also used to sell tickets to a boxing tournament in New York City. ⁵People "paid" for the tickets with various items, including mattresses, baseball bats, Bibles, and jigsaw puzzles.

The selection's main pattern of organization is _____ (write **list** or **time**).

10. ¹The Siberian tiger (the largest living cat in the world) will creep up to within thirty to eighty feet of its prey. ²It then pounces and grabs the animal—usually deer or wild pig—by the nape of the neck, keeping its back feet planted firmly on the ground. ³The bite on the neck kills small prey. ⁴Larger prey must be brought to the ground and then killed by a suffocating bite to the throat. ⁵Next, the tiger drags its meal to a safe place, usually near water. ⁶After eating until it is full, the tiger covers up what remains of the carcass, saving it for later, and then goes to sleep.

The selection's main pattern of organization is _____ (write **list** or **time**).

RELATIONSHIPS I: Test 2

1. [1]To make an unusual box, glue together all the pages of an old book you don't intend to read. [2]After the glue is dry, hollow out a large space in the block of pages.

   The time transition used is _____ (*write one word*).

2. [1]Alcoholics Anonymous is a well-known self-help group. [2]Another such group is Weight Watchers.

   The addition transition used is _____ (*write one word*).

3. [1]There are several characteristics of good daycare. [2]First of all, small groups of children are important.

   The addition transition used is _____ (*write three words*).

4. [1]One freshman irritated our history teacher, Mr. Jackson. [2]Often, she interrupted his lectures with unrelated questions and comments.

   The time transition used is _____ (*write one word*).

5. [1]Sports psychologists can help sports teams in various ways. [2]They can help select team members according to personality types. [3]Furthermore, they are able to help members improve their concentration.

   The addition transition used is _____ (*write one word*).

6. [1]Humans' fear of sharks has led to various types of protection from sharks. [2]The Navy, for example, has used dark dye as a curtain to confuse the fish. [3]It also has given sailors floating bags to hide in if they were shipwrecked near sharks. [4]Another type of protection is a metal cage, which scientists use when they wish to study the natural environment. [5]And one diver tried a wet suit made of metal chain.

   The selection's main pattern of organization is _____ (*write **list** or **time***).

7. [1]The Dutch established New Netherland in North America in 1621. [2]By 1660, the colony's population pushed toward 8,000. [3]However, in 1664, the colony's fortunes changed. [4]That year, the English king gave his brother, James, the Duke of York, title to all Dutch lands in North America. [5]There was one obvious condition: the lands must be conquered. [6]James then quickly hired someone to organize a small invasion fleet. [7]In August 1664, the ships appeared before New Amsterdam, the capital of New Netherland, on the southern end of Manhattan Island. [8]However, the Dutch governor failed to rally support, so with hardly a shot, New Netherland became the Duke of York's province. [9]He called it New York.

   The selection's main pattern of organization is _____ (*write **list** or **time***).

(Continues on next page)

8. ¹It is obvious that music is entertaining. ²However, music also has more practical uses. ³First of all, you can energize your exercise routine by using music with a steady beat. ⁴According to one study, music increases people's strength during aerobic workouts. ⁵Another practical effect of music is to improve learning. ⁶A researcher found that thirty-six students scored eight to nine points higher on a certain IQ test after listening to Mozart for ten minutes. ⁷Music can also be helpful during stressful medical procedures. ⁸For example, calming music has a positive effect on patients recovering from surgery.

The selection's main pattern of organization is _____ *(write list or time)*.

9. ¹The first two years of an infant's life are a time of dramatic physical, social, and emotional growth. ²By four months, infants are already beginning to learn about themselves. ³During this period, looking in a mirror will fascinate an infant. ⁴Between four and eight months, infants are able to express a wide range of emotions in more elaborate ways. ⁵Gurgles, coos, wails, and cries all become specific signals of certain emotions. ⁶Between eight and twelve months, infants' increased ability to crawl allows them greater social interaction. ⁷Between twelve and eighteen months, most toddlers begin to push for independence in making basic choices and performing simple tasks. ⁸Finally, between eighteen and twenty-four months, the toddler begins to develop the idea of a self. ⁹Words such as "I," "mine," and "me" now become important.

The selection's main pattern of organization is _____ *(write list or time)*.

10. ¹Social scientists have learned several things about our social roles. ²First, we aren't born with a knowledge of roles. ³We learn to meet social expectations much the same way we learn to ride a bicycle. ⁴Also, roles are only generalized guidelines for behavior. ⁵While they give us an idea of how to perform in a given situation, they don't spell out every move. ⁶Most college students, for example, need time to figure out how to be a student. ⁷Being a student involves more than enrolling for classes; students must act, dress, and even think in particular ways. ⁸Third, people have multiple roles to play. ⁹This means they must be skillful in moving between roles. ¹⁰An intern in a hospital, for instance, must be a number of different people: ¹¹At work, he or she is a doctor; at home, a husband or wife; at a party, a friend or neighbor.

The selection's main pattern of organization is _____ *(write list or time)*.

RELATIONSHIPS II: Test 1

Read each item, and then answer the question about relationships in the space provided. Write in either the transition or the pattern of organization.

1. [1]Many people view criticism negatively. [2]But if we review it calmly, we can use criticism to improve ourselves.

   The contrast transition used is _____ (write one word).

2. [1]We were impressed by the equipment at the newspaper plant. [2]For instance, there was a camera there the size of the average person's bathroom.

   The illustration transition used is _____ (write two words).

3. [1]There will be a growing number of older Americans in the 21st century. [2]Therefore, the nursing and home health care fields are also expected to grow.

   The cause and effect transition used is _____ (write one word).

4. Like the human female, the female tiger shark nourishes her young inside her body for about nine months.

   The comparison transition used is _____ (write one word).

5. [1]After a knockout punch, the victim's blood pools in the abdomen. [2]Thus there is less blood in the brain, and the victim loses consciousness.

   The cause and effect transition used is _____ (write one word).

6. [1]Americans seem to have conflicting feelings about drugs. [2]On the one hand, we disapprove of drug abuse, and we support "just say no" campaigns. [3]In contrast, we surround ourselves with messages in favor of two legal drugs: tobacco and alcohol.

   The selection's main pattern of organization is _____
   (write **def and example**, or **comparison**, or **contrast**, or **cause and effect**).

7. [1]Loud noise can have some serious effects on your health. [2]For example, being exposed to loud noise for long periods may increase tension. [3]This increased tension can lead to high blood pressure.

   The selection's main pattern of organization is _____
   (write **def and example**, or **comparison**, or **contrast**, or **cause and effect**).

(Continues on next page)

8. [1]A good speech and a good essay are similar. [2]Both begin with an introduction that grabs the audience's attention and tells what the piece is about. [3]In both, the body of the presentation should be clear and informative. [4]Finally, both end with a satisfying conclusion.

The selection's main pattern of organization is _____
(write **def and example**, or **comparison**, or **contrast**, or **cause and effect**).

9. [1]Every society has standards of behavior it considers proper. [2]Those standards are called norms. [3]Norms in American society, for instance, include men not wearing skirts and "Thou shalt not steal."

The selection's main pattern of organization is _____
(write **def and example**, or **comparison**, or **contrast**, or **cause and effect**).

10. [1]There are several reasons why the "mall concept" became popular in the early 1970s with both shoppers and store owners. [2]Buyers came to malls because of plentiful, nearby parking. [3]They also liked the convenience of being able to shop at more than one store in the same place. [4]Store owners found that being in a mall increased business because so many people passed their doors.

The selection's main pattern of organization is _____
(write **def and example**, or **comparison**, or **contrast**, or **cause and effect**).

RELATIONSHIPS II: Test 2

Read each item, and then answer the question about relationships in the space provided. Write in either the transition or the pattern of organization.

1. Because certain regions of the Amazon River flood every year, the ants that live there build their nests in trees.

   The cause and effect transition used is _____ *(write one word).*

2. There are many ways to show the elderly they are not forgotten, including regular phone calls and help with chores.

   The illustration transition used is _____ *(write one word).*

3. [1]The French government recruits quality preschool teachers by giving students a free education and a living allowance while they study. [2]As a result, France has one of the best preschool systems in the world.

   The cause and effect transition used is _____ *(write three words).*

4. The weather and soil in California's Napa Valley are similar to those in the famous French wine regions.

   The comparison signal used is _____ *(write one word).*

5. [1]Aptitude tests and achievement tests measure two quite different things. [2]Aptitude tests measure a person's ability to succeed in a given area. [3]Achievement tests show a person's actual progress at present.

   The contrast signal used is _____ *(write one word).*

6. [1]Have you ever wondered why people say "Bless you" after someone sneezes? [2]Some say the reason for blessing someone who sneezes goes back to the sixth century. [3]It was during this time that the deadly Black Death was raging through Europe. [4]The Black Death, or bubonic plague, didn't kill its victims without warning. [5]Instead, symptoms of the disease included rashes, swelling, and telltale fits of sneezing. [6]Because death so often followed sneezing, people began to say, "Bless you"—a final blessing.

   The selection's main pattern of organization is _____
   *(write **def and example**, or **comparison**, or **contrast**, or **cause and effect**).*

(Continues on next page)

7. [1]In her book *The Plug-In Drug,* author Marie Winn states that people who watch too much TV are like alcoholics. [2]Just as four or five drinks can make people forget their troubles, so can watching one television program after another. [3]Both alcohol and TV can turn excessive users into passive creatures, unwilling or unable to deal with reality. [4]Another similarity is that both alcoholics and TV addicts think that they are in control of their lives. [5]"I can stop drinking whenever I want," the alcoholic says, reaching for another Scotch or a can of beer. [6]"Sure, I'd like to go for a walk or look for a better job," the TV addict says, reaching for the remote control or the latest issue of *TV Guide.* [7]"But first I've got to see what's on TV today."

The selection's main pattern of organization is _____
(write **def and example,** or **comparison,** or **contrast,** or **cause and effect**).

8. [1]*Attachment* is the term used to describe an emotional tie with another person. [2]In young children, attachment is seen in their seeking closeness to the caregiver. [3]At twelve months, for instance, many infants cling tightly to a parent when frightened or expecting separation. [4]Reunited, they shower the parent with smiles and hugs. [5]Among the early social responses—love, fear, aggression—the first and greatest is this bond of love.

The selection's main pattern of organization is _____
(write **def and example,** or **comparison,** or **contrast,** or **cause and effect**).

9. [1]Flathead River and Lake in Montana have been changed by the introduction of opossum shrimp. [2]Between 1968 and 1975, the tiny shrimp were added to the Flathead waters. [3]The shrimp ate many of the small creatures at the bottom of the system's food chain, causing major reductions in the numbers of those creatures. [4]At the same time, mineral nutrients were changing because of the presence of the shrimp. [5]As a result, populations of algae began to increase.

The selection's main pattern of organization is _____
(write **def and example,** or **comparison,** or **contrast,** or **cause and effect**).

10. [1]A circular table is better for a working group than an oblong table. [2]Being seated in a circle increases participant motivation to speak. [3]Contrast the seeming equality of participants seated in a circle with those seated at an oblong table. [4]At an oblong table, people at the ends will be seen as having higher status—and thus be encouraged to lead. [5]Also, those sitting at the corners will tend to speak less than those at the ends or in the middle. [6]In the circle arrangement, on the other hand, sight lines are better. [7]Everyone can see everyone else. [8]And, at least in terms of seating position, everyone has equal status.

The selection's main patterns of organization are cause and effect and

_____ (write **def and example,** or **comparison,**
or **contrast**).

INFERENCES: Test 1

In the space provided, write the letter of the inference that is most firmly based on the given information in each selection.

___ 1. [1]There's a big difference between an urban sky and a country sky. [2]In the country, there are no bright lights to overpower the starlight.
  A. It is better to bring children up in the country than in the city.
  B. In the country, people can see more of the stars in the sky than they can in the city.
  C. There are actually more stars above the country than above the city.

___ 2. A British researcher found that blind people have vivid, visual dreams.
  A. Blind people dream more than others.
  B. We can "see" with our mind and imagination.
  C. People who are not blind do not have vivid dreams.

___ 3. [1]Curitaba, a city of 1.6 million in southern Brazil, has less car traffic—and the pollution it causes—than other cities. [2]The city has a seventy-five-mile network of bike paths and a very efficient low-fare bus system. [3]Curitaba is also one of the world's greenest cities. It has more than a thousand parks and plazas.
  A. Most Brazilians do not own cars.
  B. Taxes in Curitaba are probably very low.
  C. A large network of bike paths and efficient low-fare buses make it easier for people to get around without cars.

___ 4. [1]Some psychologists have commented that more time is spent preparing people for a driver's license than for a marriage license. [2]As a result, what people expect in marriage is often not realistic. [3]And the changing roles of males and females have made marriages even more complicated.
  A. The psychologists feel that marriage is a natural state for which we really need no preparation.
  B. The psychologists feel that too much time is spent in preparing people for a driver's license.
  C. The psychologists feel that married couples are more likely to be happy if they are educated about marriage.

___ 5. [1]It is easy to write down whatever comes into your head without any editing. [2]No wonder author Gertrude Stein once apologized to a friend, "Forgive me for writing such a long letter. [3]I didn't have time to write a short one."
  A. People should write letters more often.
  B. Writing a short letter or essay may be difficult because it is hard to think of a good topic to write about.
  C. It takes time and effort to edit out repetition and create an organized, effective piece of writing.

(Continues on next page)

___ 6. ¹The workplace has become highly computerized. ²Most large organizations now keep track of payroll and inventory with computer software. ³More and more, secretaries are expected to be familiar with word-processing programs. ⁴People used to assemble all parts of an automobile or appliance, but computer-controlled robots now help do the work.

A. Before long, there will be no need at all for humans in the workplace.

B. Learning how to use computers can increase one's chances of getting a job.

C. Nothing has changed the workplace more than computers have.

___ 7. ¹People develop and change as they grow older. ²If you've ever reread a diary entry or a letter you wrote some years ago, you may well have done so with a sense of amazement. ³"Is that the way I thought then? ⁴This could have been written by someone else." ⁵We often receive a similar shock at a reunion of our high-school class. ⁶We may find that the boy voted "most likely to succeed" never again achieved the success he knew in school and that the mousiest girl in the class may now be an attractive, successful executive.

A. Our thoughts and feelings are not changed very much by our experiences.

B. People's futures may be quite different from their pasts.

C. Very successful high-school students rarely become very successful adults.

___ 8. ¹In Africa, chimpanzees are captured to provide entertainment for tourists. ²The females are killed, and their young are taken and put on exhibit. ³Tourists who pay to have their pictures taken with a chimp are usually unaware that it will be killed when it is older.

A. Tourists probably know that the chimps' mothers have been killed.

B. Baby chimps are harder to handle than adult chimps.

C. The female chimps are probably killed because otherwise they would fight anyone trying to take their children.

___ 9. ¹Modern light bulbs, TV, shift work, and social activities have greatly interfered with people's sleep patterns. ²Teenagers typically need eight or nine hours sleep. ³Today, they average nearly two hours less sleep a night than their counterparts of a century ago. ⁴Many fill this need by using homeroom for their first nap and after-lunch study hall for a slumber party. ⁵As one sleep researcher put it, "The national sleep debt is larger and more important than the national debt."

A. Today's adults' sleep patterns are no different from the patterns of adults a century ago.

B. The author of the selection feels that the purpose of homerooms should be to sleep.

C. Before modern advances, people were more likely to go to sleep when it became dark outside.

___10. ¹Much of our everyday conversation is ceremony. ²We ask others, "How are you?" without expecting a full account of their recent medical history. ³We often hear and see things in a mindless fashion because what we say is far less important than the fact that we are still talking to one another.

A. Language should never be used in a mindless fashion.

B. Communicating nothing more than friendliness is one good use of language.

C. The words we say are always more important than how we say them.

INFERENCES: Test 2

In the space provided, write the letter of the inference that is most firmly based on the given information in each selection.

___ 1. [1]When the Communists took over Russia, the former czar and his family, the Romanovs, were supposedly all executed. [2]But in 1920, a young woman was fished out of a canal in Berlin. [3]She claimed to be Anastasia, the daughter of the former czar. [4]She said she had been wounded in the execution and was helped to escape by a member of the firing squad. [5]While evidence existed for and against her story, historians were uncertain about its truth. [6]However, scientists recently discovered through the woman's genes that she was unrelated to the Romanovs.
  A. The Romanovs were executed long after 1920.
  B. Nobody ever believed the young woman's story that she was Anastasia.
  C. Science can help to solve mysteries.

___ 2. [1]In hot weather, we need to be especially careful about food storage to avoid the risk of food poisoning, caused by bacteria. [2]Highly perishable items like milk and mayonnaise should be kept in the coldest part of the refrigerator. [3]Meat, poultry, and fish which will not be eaten within two days from purchase should be stored in the freezer. [4]Perishable foods left out for more than two hours should be thrown away.
  A. The food we buy has often not been well cared for by the supermarket.
  B. Bacteria grow more quickly in a warm environment than in a cold one.
  C. It is difficult to avoid food poisoning.

___ 3. [1]There are several types of crime. [2]The type people fear the most is crimes of violence against people, including, of course, murder and rape. [3]The second type is crimes against property, in which a criminal damages or steals something belonging to another person. [4]Next are crimes without victims. [5]Those who suffer from these crimes are the criminals themselves, including gamblers and prostitutes. [6]Finally, there's white-collar crime, crime committed on the job by respected people in responsible positions.
  A. The author believes that white-collar crimes are worse than crimes against property.
  B. People fear violence more than they fear loss of money.
  C. A kidnapping is a white-collar crime.

(Continues on next page)

___ 4. [1]The idea of romantic love originated in Europe during the Middle Ages. [2]It was then described as a pure and holy emotion. [3]In England, it wasn't until the end of the 1600s that love was considered essential for an ideal marriage. [4]In India, films about couples who marry for love (rather than because their parents arrange the match) have become common only in the last several years. [5]According to one report, only 50 percent of the women and 33 percent of the men in Russia said they marry for love. [6]Most said they marry because of loneliness, shared interests, or pregnancy. [7]In contrast, most Americans (87 percent) say they believe love is essential to a good marriage.

A. Falling in love before marriage is the only natural human pattern.

B. A couple whose marriage was arranged will never learn to love each other.

C. Marrying for love has become more common through the centuries.

___ 5. [1]Various experiments reveal that there are several factors involved in whether or not people help others. [2]One factor is how deserving the victim is thought to be. [3]This was shown in an experiment in which people pretended to be in need of help. [4]If they carried a cane, they were helped more promptly than if they carried a liquor bottle. [5]Another factor is gender. [6]Women tend to help both men and women equally. [7]Men, on the other hand, are more likely to help women. [8]Last, appearance plays a part—people are more likely to help others who are dressed like themselves.

A. People who drink a lot are often seen as having brought their problems on themselves.

B. People are more likely to help someone they think is quite different from themselves.

C. Men feel other men don't deserve their help.

___ 6. [1]One of the luckiest mistakes of all time was made by Christopher Columbus. [2]In his time, educated people knew the world was round, but they didn't know how big it was. [3]One theory, which Columbus believed, said that the world was much smaller than it really is. [4]Thus, Columbus thought he wouldn't have to sail too far west from Spain to reach Japan. [5]When he landed at Cuba, he thought he'd found Japan. [6]If he had known that Japan was actually more than twelve thousand miles west of Spain, he might never have tried to sail that way—and he never would have reached America.

A. Christopher Columbus is honored in the United States for something he never intended to do.

B. Everyone in Columbus's day knew that the world was round.

C. In Columbus's day, nobody had yet heard of Japan.

(Continues on next page)

____ 7. [1]We often hear that opposites attract. [2]However, research shows that it is more often the case that birds of a feather flock together. [3]People generally seek out others who are similar to themselves in appearance and actions. [4]If you doubt this, ask yourself how willing you are to communicate with someone whose behavior is totally different from yours. [5]Or ask yourself what your first reaction is to people who look strange. [6]Most people find it difficult to deal with the odd or unusual.

A. It is impossible to be friends with someone who is very unlike yourself.

B. Most friendships are quite weak.

C. We tend to be more comfortable with people like ourselves.

____ 8. [1]Did you ever wonder why birthday cakes are almost always round and lit with candles? [2]Here is how the tradition started. [3]The ancient Greeks believed there was a goddess of the moon named Artemis. [4]They celebrated her birthday each year by bringing a cake to a place dedicated as her temple. [5]The cakes were round and ringed with candles, to make them look like glowing full moons. [6]The tradition of round birthday cakes with candles on them persists to this day in many nations around the world.

A. Birthday cakes today are much better than those of ancient Greece.

B. Traditions can last for centuries after their origins are long forgotten.

C. The Greeks celebrated all of their gods' birthdays with round cakes.

____ 9. [1]Your friend's new restaurant is a big success. [2]All her hard work and planning are really paying off as customers flock to dine there. [3]She's thrilled, of course. [4]And you are thrilled for her, aren't you? [5]What? [6]You feel miserable? [7]If so, your feelings aren't that unusual. [8]Many people are secretly pleased when their friends fail at something, and they are tortured by envy when they succeed. [9]Psychologists say these unpleasant feelings have a lot to do with one's self-image. [10]People who have trouble sincerely enjoying someone else's success probably don't think very much of themselves. [11]When a friend does well, it makes those people feel less important by comparison.

A. Someone with a strong self-image is more likely to be happy about a friend's success.

B. Successful people never have true friends.

C. "Never trust your friends" is good advice.

____10. [1]People in the United States and other Western countries learn "It's the squeaky wheel that gets the grease." [2]In other words, those people who get what they want will be the ones who draw the most attention to themselves. [3]People with this Western view seek independence. [4]However, in Eastern cultures, people learn "The nail that sticks up shall be hammered down." [5]People with this Eastern view emphasize people's dependence on each other.

A. People with an Eastern point of view are more likely to call attention to themselves.

B. People with a Western point of view are more likely to want to stand out from the crowd.

C. There is really no difference between the Western and Eastern points of view.

Name _____

Section _____ Date _____

SCORE: (Number correct) × 10 = _____%

IMPLIED MAIN IDEAS: Test 1

In the space provided, write the letter of the general idea that best covers each group of specific ideas. Remember that the correct general idea will not be too narrow or too broad. It will describe what the specific ideas have in common.

___ 1. *Specific ideas:* biologist, chemist, geologist, physicist

The general idea is
A. university researchers.
B. workers.
C. scientists.

___ 2. *Specific ideas: Time, Newsweek, People, Good Housekeeping*

The general idea is
A. magazines.
B. news magazines.
C. publications.

___ 3. *Specific ideas:* vanilla fudge, chocolate, peach, strawberry

The general idea is
A. flavors.
B. ice cream flavors.
C. fruit flavors.

___ 4. *Specific ideas:* rifle, pistol, bomb, revolver

The general idea is
A. handguns.
B. guns.
C. weapons.

___ 5. *Specific ideas:* czar, prime minister, king, president

The general idea is
A. dictators.
B. national leaders.
C. elected officials.

___ 6. *Specific ideas:* inch, mile, yard, gallon

The general idea is
A. measurements.
B. distance measurements.
C. volume measurements.

(Continues on next page)

_____ 7. *Specific ideas:* hot-water bottle, thermometer, pills, bedpan

The general idea is
A. medications.
B. household items.
C. sickroom items.

_____ 8. *Specific ideas:* knitting, crocheting, woodcarving, embroidery

The general idea is
A. needlework.
B. crafts.
C. household chores.

_____ 9. *Specific ideas:* airplanes, birds, clouds, moon

The general idea is
A. things that fly.
B. things with wings.
C. things that can be seen in the sky.

_____10. *Specific ideas:* "No," "Absolutely not," "Never," "Over my dead body"

The general idea is
A. replies.
B. refusals.
C. statements.

IMPLIED MAIN IDEAS: Test 2

In the space provided, write the letter of the implied main idea of each paragraph.

____ 1. [1]In the United States, about half of the apples grown are eaten fresh. [2]About a fifth are used for jelly, juice, vinegar, and apple butter. [3]And another fifth go for apple sauce and canned filling for pie.

    A. Americans use fruits in various ways.

    B. In the United States, apples are used in several ways.

    C. About the same percentage of apples are used for jelly as are used for apple sauce and canned pie filling.

____ 2. [1]One common guideline for a healthy diet is to eat a variety of foods—doctors say that is the best way to get the nutrients you need. [2]A second common guideline is to choose foods that are low in fat. [3]This means avoiding such things as french fries, potato chips, and cheeseburgers. [4]Third, eat plenty of fresh fruits and vegetables. [5]Fourth, eat whole-grain foods such as cereals and breads—but don't slather them with butter! [6]In addition, hold down your intake of sugars and salt. [7]Finally, say most experts, if you drink alcohol at all, drink lightly.

    A. Fats are bad for your health.

    B. There are several common guidelines to help you choose a healthful diet.

    C. Eating a healthful diet will prevent disease and make you live longer.

____ 3. [1]Babies with very low birth weight have trouble maintaining a normal body temperature because they do not have enough body fat to keep them warm. [2]Also, they are less able to ward off infection, and so they may become seriously ill. [3]They may be too weak even to suck, so they have to be fed by artificial means—increasing their exposure to infection. [4]In addition, their lungs might not be strong enough to let them breathe properly.

    A. Babies with low birth weight are at risk of several problems.

    B. There are several reasons why babies are born weighing less than normal.

    C. Good prenatal care is the best way to avoid low birth weight babies.

____ 4. [1]The Center for Disease Control in Atlanta, Georgia, has conducted wide-scale surveys in eleven states to determine teenagers' knowledge about AIDS. [2]Half of the teens surveyed believe a person can get AIDS through giving blood. [3]Almost three-quarters of teenagers think that AIDS can be gotten from a simple blood test. [4]And half believe that the disease can be easily contracted from a public toilet. [5]None of these beliefs is well-founded.

    A. According to one survey, many teens have a poor understanding of how people get AIDS.

    B. The Center for Disease Control conducted a survey to discover teens' knowledge about AIDS.

    C. Teenagers have a poor understanding of sexually transmitted diseases.

(Continues on next page)

_____ 5. [1]Before they can say any words, babies communicate by making a variety of sounds. [2]They start by crying. [3]Then they progress to cooing when they are happy, squealing, gurgling, and making long "oohs" and "aahs." [4]At about six months they babble, repeating syllables such as "buh" and "muh." [5]Next they start to imitate sounds they hear, even though they don't seem to understand these sounds. [6]At the next stage, they string such sounds together in a way that is almost speechlike. [7]At about age 1, they say their first meaningful word—usually "mama" or "dada." [8]Soon they use many words, and at about eighteen months they begin to make combinations of words, forming simple sentences.

    A. Babies are able to communicate before they can actually speak.
    B. Babies coo and babble when they are happy.
    C. Babies learn to speak in several stages.

_____ 6. [1]According to scientists, cockroaches evolved about 300 million years ago, which means they saw the dinosaurs come and go and later watched people emerge on Earth. [2]If you wonder how such little creatures have lasted so long, consider the fact that they can live in a refrigerator or in extreme heat. [3]They can develop resistance to poisons faster than scientists can develop new ones. [4]And they can live for two months on water alone or go for five months without water. [5]Furthermore, they are quick to escape from danger. [6]The takeoff time for a threatened cockroach has been timed at 54/1000th of a second.

    A. Cockroaches evolved about 300 million years ago.
    B. Cockroaches can live in a wide variety of temperatures and quickly develop resistance to poisons.
    C. Cockroaches have survived for millions of years because they can adapt to a wide variety of circumstances and react quickly to danger.

_____ 7. [1]When you are warned to be careful and pay attention, you may be told to "mind your p's and q's!" [2]Why p's and q's? [3]One explanation says that barkeepers used to keep a written record of their customers' debts. [4]The record would state how many pints (p's) or quarts (q's) of ale the customer owed payment for. [5]Sometimes the barkeep would tell patrons to mind their p's and q's, meaning to pay what they owed. [6]But a different explanation says that the expression was born in the print shop. [7]Printers have always had trouble setting letters that are mirror images of one another, like _p_'s and _q_'s or _b_'s and _d_'s. [8]"Mind your p's and q's" may have been a way of reminding a printer to be careful while setting type.

    A. "Mind your p's and q's" means to be careful and pay attention.
    B. There are two interesting explanations for the phrase "mind your p's and q's."
    C. Printers have always had trouble setting letters that are mirror images of one another, like _p_'s and _q_'s.

(Continues on next page)

___ 8. [1]The tobacco industry spends more than $500 million a year on advertising. [2]No wonder—there's a lot of money at stake. [3]At one point, Reynolds Tobacco estimated that if every smoker smoked one less cigarette a day for a year, it would cost the industry $450 million. [4]Cigarette manufacturers aren't the only ones who want to see people smoking. [5]Many Third World countries depend on income from cigarette taxes. [6]And throughout the world, tobacco growers receive financial help from their governments that they would not receive for other crops.

    A. There are many who benefit financially from tobacco sales and thus want people to continue smoking.

    B. One tobacco company estimated that it would cost the industry millions if every smoker smoked one less cigarette a day for a year.

    C. Governments sometimes provide farmers with special financial help for growing certain crops.

___ 9. [1]We are all familiar with embarrassing slips of the tongue—for example, when the doctor asks someone, "How would you like to be killed?" instead of "billed." [2]Sigmund Freud had an explanation. [3]He said that such mistakes are the result of unconscious thoughts and feelings. [4]According to Freud, the doctor in the example may have had unconscious feelings of anger toward the patient. [5]Today, other psychologists have a different explanation. [6]These researchers note that the words in our mental dictionary can be compared to central crossing points in a spider's web. [7]When we try to say a particular word, other nearby words are also activated, mainly on the basis of meaning, sound, and grammar. [8]Thus, the doctor might possibly have said *kill* instead of *bill* because of the similarities in sound.

    A. Sigmund Freud said that slips of the tongue are due to unconscious thoughts and feelings.

    B. There are differing views on what causes slips of the tongue.

    C. Some psychologists say that slips of the tongue happen on the basis of meaning, sound, and grammar.

___10. [1]At the beginning of the nineteenth century, young children worked for a few pennies a day to help their families. [2]In Boston in 1830, children made up two-fifths of the labor force. [3]The labor of young women drove the entire cotton and woolen industries. [4]Work hours lasted from daybreak to dark, and wages were low. [5]In the spinning and weaving mills of New Jersey, children earned an average of a little more than a dollar a week. [6]By the end of the nineteenth century, the typical workweek ran to sixty hours. [7]But in some industries, such as steel, seventy-two or even eighty-four hours was common. [8]That breaks down to seven twelve-hour days a week. [9]Working conditions still frequently remained unsafe, and child labor remained common.

    A. The cotton and woolen industries of the nineteenth century depended on the work of young women.

    B. Many young people in the 1800s did not attend school.

    C. During the 1800s, an important part of the labor force was young people, who worked long hours for little pay.

THE BASICS OF ARGUMENT: Test 1

In each of the following groups, one statement is the point, and the other statements are support for the point. Write the letter of the point of the group.

____ 1. A. Huge furry spiders live in my basement.
   B. Many tiny white moths fly around in my closet.
   C. Many different insects live in my home.
   D. At night when the lights go out, cockroaches visit my kitchen.

____ 2. A. In recent decades, some businesses have been victims of false rumors.
   B. About twenty years ago, there was a false rumor that McDonald's added worms to their hamburgers.
   C. In 1991, a soap manufacturer was falsely accused of practicing devil worship.
   D. Not too long ago, someone started a rumor that cans of Pepsi contained surgical needles.

____ 3. A. Jesse was chosen by his classmates to speak at graduation.
   B. The winning goal in three of the season's soccer games was scored by Jesse.
   C. The science project Jesse entered at the school science fair took the blue ribbon.
   D. Jesse is having an outstanding senior year at school.

____ 4. A. Some people diet to the point of starvation, believing that at a normal weight, they are fat.
   B. Some people seem to never feel full and continue eating until they are enormously overweight.
   C. Eating large amounts of food, then vomiting and taking laxatives to avoid gaining weight is another eating disorder.
   D. There are several different types of eating disorders.

____ 5. A. Mrs. Dixon grows all her own vegetables and bakes her own bread.
   B. At age 87, Mrs. Dixon is remarkably active and independent.
   C. To celebrate her eighty-eighth birthday, Mrs. Dixon is planning to take a ride in a hot-air balloon.
   D. Every day, Mrs. Dixon walks downtown to pick up her mail and chat with friends.

____ 6. A. Drinking coffee at lunch or at break gives many people a little caffeine lift.
   B. Many people require a daily dose of chocolate, which contains caffeine.
   C. Many people use caffeine to get them through the day.
   D. People who don't drink coffee often have tea or a carbonated beverage, both of which can contain caffeine.

(Continues on next page)

_____ 7. A. Tanya subscribes to not just one but three daily newspapers.

      B. Tanya describes herself as a "news addict," and that's an accurate description.

      C. In the evening, Tanya tapes two news programs and watches another one live.

      D. Tanya's clock-radio is tuned to an all-news station, so news stories wake her up every day.

_____ 8. A. During the 1600s, Europeans got married for economic reasons, not love.

      B. Life in Europe during the 1600s was extremely different from life today.

      C. In Europe during the 1600s, people died young—40 was considered old age.

      D. In Europe during the 1600s, childhood often ended at age 10—when most children left home to work as servants, shepherds, and apprentices.

_____ 9. A. Watching a rental film at home is better than going to the movie theater.

      B. Renting a movie is cheaper than buying two or more tickets to a theater.

      C. When renting a movie, people do not have to put up with the long lines that moviegoers often deal with.

      D. When watching a film at home, one avoids the annoying crowds at movie theaters.

_____10. A. Since 1970, the number of people staying single in the United States has increased by 127 percent.

      B. Being single has become an increasingly popular way of life in America.

      C. From 1990 through 1996, the average age at which people first get married shifted from 22 to 26.

      D. Today, single people head 25 percent of all American households—more than ever in history.

THE BASICS OF ARGUMENT: Test 2

Each point is followed by three statements that provide logical support for the point and one statement that does not. Write the letter of the one statement that does **not** support the point.

____ 1. **Point:** My roommate is very messy.
   A. He leaves piles of dirty laundry on the floor for weeks at a time.
   B. When he cooks, he manages to spill food over the entire kitchen.
   C. His room does not have enough closet space.
   D. He throws his wet towels all over the bathroom.

____ 2. **Point:** That highway is dangerous.
   A. There are some sharp, unexpected curves on the highway.
   B. The highway is the quickest way into the city.
   C. More accidents happen on the highway each year than anywhere else in the state.
   D. There is no shoulder on the highway, leaving no room for drivers to swerve to avoid hitting other cars.

____ 3. **Point:** The new movie theater is poorly designed.
   A. There are not enough parking spaces for moviegoers.
   B. There are too few ticket windows, so lines are too long and move slowly.
   C. The rows of seats are too close together.
   D. The old theater in town shows better movies than the new one does.

____ 4. **Point:** Transferring to a new school can be difficult for kids.
   A. Many students worry that people in their new school will not like them.
   B. Students in a new school often feel lonely and miss their old friends.
   C. For most kids, the difficulty of changing schools lasts for a short time.
   D. If the new school is more advanced than the old one, the new kid may have to work especially hard to catch up.

____ 5. **Point:** Moving to a new apartment can be expensive.
   A. Most landlords require at least a month's rent as a security deposit.
   B. Many apartments have no refrigerator, so the tenant has to buy one.
   C. If tenants are moving from another apartment, they usually already have some of their own furnishings and supplies.
   D. A new apartment calls for a lot of small purchases, such as curtains and lamps.

____ 6. **Point:** My brother-in-law and I do not get along well.
   A. He and my sister got married when I was 13 and in the eighth grade.
   B. When I am eating, he often makes critical comments about my weight.
   C. He resents the fact that his wife and I still like to spend time alone without him.
   D. More than once he has told me that I am too loud and messy in his home.

(Continues on next page)

___ 7. **Point:** The world's population is growing quickly.
    A. Each year, 94 million babies are added to the world's population.
    B. Today it takes eleven years to produce one billion people; it once took five hundred years for this to happen.
    C. In many countries, including Japan, the population is actually decreasing.
    D. At the current rate of world population growth, the population will double in size in only forty years.

___ 8. **Point:** The department store in town is not well run.
    A. The store frequently runs out of an advertised item and has to give away rain checks for it.
    B. In February when the weather was still wet and cold, the store started offering nothing but summer clothing.
    C. The aisles are so dirty that if an item falls on the floor, no one wants to pick it up.
    D. Many clerks and cashiers there are mothers who work while their children are in school.

___ 9. **Point:** Exposure to sunlight can have both positive and negative health effects.
    A. When exposed to sunlight, the skin produces Vitamin D, which is essential for good health.
    B. Some parts of the world see as little as four hours of sunlight per day.
    C. In some people, the lack of sunlight produces a disorder that includes depression, weight gain, and anxiety.
    D. Becoming tanned or sunburned can lead to the development of skin cancers in many people.

___ 10. **Point:** My daughter benefits from her experience at daycare.
    A. She has been attending daycare since she was eighteen months old.
    B. Dealing with other children at daycare has helped her learn to share, to cooperate, and to consider other people's feelings.
    C. Through the stories, rhymes, and songs she has learned at daycare, she has developed a good vocabulary and love of music.
    D. Making new friends at daycare has helped her become confident and outgoing.

COMBINED SKILLS: Test 1

After reading the passage, write the letter of the best answer to each question.

[1]There are several types of experiences that influence how people feel about being touched. [2]Our childhood experiences are one thing that affect our attitudes towards touching. [3]Little girls, for example, are generally kissed and cuddled more than little boys. [4]As a result, women often like touching more than men. [5]Our feelings about being touched also depend upon our cultural background. [6]Latin Americans and southern Europeans, for instance, casually touch each other far more than northern Europeans and most Americans. [7]Finally, social context influences our willingness to touch and be touched. [8]For example, even men who are generally wary about touching may hug one another at an exciting sporting event.

____ 1. In sentence 7, the word *context* means
    A. power.
    B. situation.
    C. delay.
    D. disappointment.

____ 2. In sentence 8, the word *wary* means
    A. without knowledge.
    B. angry.
    C. unsure.
    D. violent.

____ 3. The topic sentence of the passage is sentence
    A. 1.
    B. 2.
    C. 5.
    D. 8.

____ 4. Latin Americans are more used to touching than
    A. southern Europeans.
    B. Americans.
    C. men at an exciting game.
    D. all of the above.

____ 5. According to the author,
    A. Latin Americans casually touch each other far more than southern Europeans do.
    B. Latin Americans and southern Europeans are kinder than North Americans.
    C. willingness to touch casually is greater in the southern areas mentioned than in the northern areas.
    D. social context is a stronger influence on behavior than cultural background and childhood experiences.

(Continues on next page)

_____ 6. The relationship between sentences 3 and 4 is one of
  A. time.
  B. addition.
  C. cause and effect.
  D. comparison.

_____ 7. The relationship of sentence 7 to the sentences before it is one of
  A. time.
  B. addition.
  C. cause and effect.
  D. contrast.

_____ 8. The passage
  A. lists types of touch.
  B. discusses causes and effects of touch.
  C. presents a series of historical events relating to touch.
  D. lists things that influence how much people touch one another.

_____ 9. Specifically, the major supporting details of the passage are
  A. Americans, Latin Americans, and Europeans.
  B. childhood and adulthood.
  C. childhood experiences, cultural background, and social context.
  D. little girls and boys, Americans and others, and sporting events.

_____ 10. We can conclude that
  A. little boys and girls are treated much the same worldwide.
  B. the way we are brought up may influence what we're comfortable with as adults.
  C. southern European boys are brought up exactly the same way as northern European boys.
  D. Latin American women like touching less than American women do.

COMBINED SKILLS: Test 2

After reading the passage, write the letter of the best answer to each question.

[1]Many people believe that describing their true feelings reveals too much about them. [2]If you tell people what hurts you, you risk their using the information against you when they want to hurt you on purpose. [3]Nevertheless, the potential benefits of revealing your true feelings far outweigh the risks. [4]For instance, imagine Pete has a nickname for you that you dislike. [5]If you tell Pete that you are upset when he uses that nickname, he does have the option of calling you by that name when he wants to hurt you, but he is more likely to stop calling you by that name. [6]If, on the other hand, you don't describe your feelings to Pete, he's probably going to continue calling you by that name simply because he doesn't know any better. [7]By saying nothing, you support his behavior. [8]The level of risk varies with each situation, but you will more often improve a relationship by describing feelings than be hurt by doing so.

1. In sentence 3, the word *potential* means
   A. imaginary.
   B. possible.
   C. harmful.
   D. minor.

2. In sentence 5, the word *option* means
   A. answer.
   B. question.
   C. feeling.
   D. choice.

3. The main idea of the passage is first stated in sentence
   A. 1.
   B. 2.
   C. 3.
   D. 4.

4. The main idea of the passage is repeated in sentence
   A. 5.
   B. 6.
   C. 7.
   D. 8.

5. According to the author,
   A. telling what hurts you is not a good idea.
   B. the way to reveal feelings is to describe them.
   C. disguising feelings is sometimes a good idea.
   D. revealing feelings will never hurt you.

(Continues on next page)

6. The relationship of sentence 3 to sentence 2 is one of
   A. addition.
   B. time.
   C. contrast.
   D. illustration.

7. The relationship of sentences 4–7 to sentence 3 is one of
   A. addition.
   B. time.
   C. contrast.
   D. an example.

8. We can conclude the author feels that
   A. people often wish to hurt others.
   B. many people are too sensitive.
   C. we sometimes have to take risks in our relationships with others.
   D. you will probably get hurt if you describe how things make you feel.

9. The author suggests that if you don't reveal your feelings,
   A. you will lose friends.
   B. you are lying.
   C. you will hurt others' feelings.
   D. whatever bothers you is likely to continue.

10. The author would probably say that if a friend constantly interrupts you, you should
    A. end the friendship.
    B. interrupt your friend too.
    C. ignore the interruptions.
    D. tell the friend how the interruptions make you feel.

ANSWERS TO THE TESTS IN THE SECOND TEST BANK

DICTIONARY USE: Test 1

1. B
2. B
3. C
4. B
5. B
6. B
7. A
8. C
9. A
10. A

DICTIONARY USE: Test 2

1. A
2. B
3. A
4. C
5. B
6. C
7. A
8. C
9. B
10. C

VOCABULARY IN CONTEXT: Test 1

1. C
2. D
3. C
4. C
5. D
6. A
7. B
8. A
9. B
10. D

VOCABULARY IN CONTEXT: Test 2

1. D
2. C
3. C
4. A
5. B
6. A
7. A
8. B
9. A
10. C

MAIN IDEAS: Test 1

1. Europeans
2. road surface
3. track and field event
4. wall coverings
5. fish
6. game
7. punctuation mark
8. aircraft
9. home
10. misfortune

MAIN IDEAS: Test 2

1. A
2. C
3. B
4. B
5. B
6. A
7. B
8. B
9. C
10. A

SUPPORTING DETAILS: Test 1

1. 2
2. 2
3. 3
4. 2
5. 3
6. 3
7. 4
8. 2
9. 3
10. 3

SUPPORTING DETAILS: Test 2

1. B
2. A
3. A
4. A
5. B
6. B
7. A
8. C
9. A
10. C

LOCATIONS OF MAIN IDEAS: Test 1

1. 2
2. 1
3. 7
4. 2
5. 3
6. 5
7. 2
8. 3
9. 6
10. 2

LOCATIONS OF MAIN IDEAS: Test 2

1. 2
2. 1
3. 3
4. 1
5. 5
6. 5
7. 2
8. 7
9. 2
10. 7

RELATIONSHIPS I: Test 1

1. After
2. Another
3. when
4. Furthermore
5. First of all
6. list
7. time
8. time
9. list
10. time

RELATIONSHIPS I: Test 2

1. After
2. Another
3. First of all
4. Often
5. Furthermore
6. list
7. time
8. list
9. time
10. list

RELATIONSHIPS II: Test 1

1. But	6. contrast
2. For instance	7. cause and effect
3. Therefore	8. comparison
4. Like	9. def and example
5. Thus	10. cause and effect

RELATIONSHIPS II: Test 2

1. Because	6. cause and effect
2. including	7. comparison
3. As a result	8. def and example
4. similar	9. cause and effect
5. different	10. contrast

INFERENCES: Test 1

1. B	6. B
2. B	7. B
3. C	8. C
4. C	9. C
5. C	10. B

INFERENCES: Test 2

1. C	6. A
2. B	7. C
3. B	8. B
4. C	9. A
5. A	10. B

IMPLIED MAIN IDEAS: Test 1

1. C	6. A
2. A	7. C
3. B	8. B
4. C	9. C
5. B	10. B

IMPLIED MAIN IDEAS: Test 2

1. B	6. C
2. B	7. B
3. A	8. A
4. A	9. B
5. C	10. C

THE BASICS OF ARGUMENT: Test 1

1. C	6. C
2. A	7. B
3. D	8. B
4. D	9. A
5. B	10. B

THE BASICS OF ARGUMENT: Test 2

1. C	6. A
2. B	7. C
3. D	8. D
4. C	9. B
5. C	10. A

COMBINED SKILLS: Test 1

1. B	6. C
2. C	7. B
3. A	8. D
4. B	9. C
5. C	10. B

COMBINED SKILLS: Test 2

1. B	6. C
2. D	7. D
3. C	8. C
4. D	9. D
5. B	10. D

Notes

Notes

Notes

Notes